THE RETREAT FROM BURMA

The Retreat from Burma

Lt. Col. Tony Mains

NEW ENGLISH LIBRARY
TIMES MIRROR

This book is dedicated to the Officers and men, British, Indian and Gurkha, who served in or with the Indian Intelligence Corps in World War II, and in particular, to my three 'Chiefs', Jock Campbell, Tony Boyce and Philip Gwyn for their invariable support and kindness.

First published in Great Britain by W. Foulsham & Co. Ltd. 1973
© Copyright Tony Mains 1973

*

FIRST NEL PAPERBACK EDITION AUGUST 1974

NEL Books are published by
New English Library Limited from Barnard's Inn, Holborn. London E.C.1.
Made and printed in Great Britain by Hunt Barnard Printing Ltd., Aylesbury, Bucks.

45001976 4

CONTENTS

MAPS AND DIAGRAMS

FOREWORD

by

The Chief of the Army Staff in India

I was asked by the author, Tony Mains, to write a foreword to his book, *The Retreat from Burma,* and I agreed to do this for two reasons. One, Tony Mains is a friend of long standing: and two, he is a fellow Gurkha. However, on reading the manuscript, I find I have a third reason, which is that this is an extremely well written account of a portion of a campaign of which I, too, have personal knowledge.

The author traces the growth of what is now the Intelligence Corps of India: strangely, prior to 1939, Intelligence and Security were just taken for granted and it took World War II for the authorities to realize the vital importance of this branch of the Service.

This book is primarily an individual account of events as seen and experienced by a comparatively junior officer and a small unit which he commanded. They were often asked to discharge duties and accept responsibilities for which they were neither organized, staffed nor trained: it speaks highly of the professional competence, initiative and enthusiasm of Tony Mains and his band of dedicated men who acquitted themselves so well and creditably under conditions which were disturbed and disorganized.

New Delhi

SHFJ MANEKSHAW
Field Marshal.

PREFACE

The idea of writing this book came to me while I was staying with the Commandant of the Indian Military Academy, in 1969. The Commandant, at that time, was Major-General 'Monty' Palit, VrC, FRGS, and he was also Colonel of my old Regiment, 9th Gurkha Rifles. Monty, who is himself the author of several books of military interest and international repute, suggested that I should write down my experiences as an Intelligence Officer of Headquarters Burma Army during the retreat of 1942, and he has since given me much advice and encouragement, for which I am greatly indebted to him.

The aim of this book is limited to an account of the day-to-day fortunes of a junior staff officer during a chaotic period of the Second World War, and includes the story of the 'last ditchers' of Rangoon which, I believe, has not yet been told in full. It is not intended to be a detailed history of the actual campaign; this has been given already in the very competent Official History, 'The War Against Japan', Volume II. However, to enable the reader to put the events narrated into their proper chronological sequence and perspective, a certain amount of the history of the campaign has been included. I am indebted, therefore, to the authors of the Official History for their clear and readable account, parts of which have been quoted when my memory was uncertain.

It must be realised that the Intelligence Services in the Indian Army prior to 1939 were very deficient and the Security Services, as later known, did not exist at all. There was no Army Intelligence School and the two-week Intelligence Courses run by the Army Commands were mainly designed to train Air Intelligence Liaison Officers for duty with the RAF Army Co-operation Squadrons in operations on the North West Frontier. Intelligence staffs were found at Divisional and Brigade Headquarters only in those formations serving on the Frontier. Staffs at higher levels were appointed from officers who had qualified at the Staff College, without any specialised Intelligence training.

The Army in India did not mobilise, as a whole, in 1939 and the early formations sent to the Middle East received their Intelligence and Security staffs from the British Army. The first Indian formation to have a proper system of Intelligence and Security cover was the force sent to Iraq in 1941, and this was followed by the Army in Burma in 1942. It seems incredible that there were no Identity cards until these were introduced in the Iraq Force and subsequently, into the Burma Army. India Command did not introduce them for general use until the winter of 1942–3.

The contrast between the conditions described in this book and the highly sophisticated Security cover existing by 1944 was very marked, for by then every formation, both on the fighting front and on the Lines of Communication, had its own Intelligence and Security staffs to direct and plan, and its Field Security Sections to carry out actual Security work.

The Government of India maintained a highly efficient Intelligence organisation known as the 'Intelligence Bureau' – as readers of 'Kim' will know, although Kipling did not call it by this, its later title. This Bureau had its main office in Delhi and branch offices in Peshawar and Quetta. It is difficult to find an exact equivalent in Britain, as it carried out both Intelligence and Security functions. It was concerned, primarily, with providing information about the tribesmen of the North West Frontier, on both sides of the

Indo–Afghanistan border and also about conditions in countries bordering on India. On the Security side, it was something of a cross between MI5 and the Special Branch of the Metropolitan Police, as it provided information regarding subversion and anti-government activity, whether originating from within or without India. It was staffed mainly by Officers of the Indian Police but Army Officers were also employed, more especially at Peshawar and Quetta. The wave of anti-Government activity in the late Twenties and early Thirties had forced the Intelligence Bureau into a revision of the arrangements existing for liaison between the Army and the Police. The outcome was the posting of 'Military Intelligence Officers' with the Civil Police at strategic and important places. Those officers originally trained at Command Intelligence Courses were seconded to the Civil Government, who gave them the rank of Additional Superintendent of Police. Their duties were to organise intelligence of anti-Government activities, acting in this respect as 'field agents' of the Intelligence Bureau and to act as liaison officers between the Army and the Police. The Intelligence Bureau covered Burma also, until the separation in 1937, but subsequent to this the Government of Burma set up its own 'Burma Defence Bureau'.

The foregoing survey indicates that such organisations as did exist, were designed either for operations on the North West Frontier or to combat anti-Government activity; Intelligence and Security organisations designed to combat the enemy were slow to materialise and in the face of enemy activity, difficult to improvise.

I

Prologue — The Move to Rangoon

This book is a personal account of my experience during the Burma Retreat of 1941. It is not intended to be a treatise on the campaign, nor to show the strategical or tactical lessons, but to recount what actually happened to a junior officer of the Security Intelligence branch of Army Headquarters. It will indicate the neglect of the security aspect of intelligence in the British Army until 1939 and in the Indian Army until much later.

The general account is written from memory but the actual sequence of the campaign has been checked with the Official History – *The War Against Japan Volume II*. My appointment was to the Intelligence Staff whereas much of the book will be about the various diverse 'odd jobs' with which my colleagues and I had to deal, owing to the breakdown of much of the normal administration during the campaign.

This narrative starts on my 28th birthday, 29 December 1941, when holding the appointment of a third grade officer of the General Staff but working in the security section of the Intelligence Branch of Headquarters Iraq Force in Baghdad, I received orders to proceed to India to take up a new and more senior Intelligence appointment in the Far East – this could have been in either Burma or Malaya but at this time, I had no knowledge of which theatre it was to be.

The references later in the narrative to the various gradings of Intelligence officers and to the various sections in which they worked, according to the staff system prevailing in the British Army at that time, requires some explanation if the non-military reader is not to be confused by the various abbreviations in common use. Intelligence was a branch of the General Staff and the abbreviation GSI referred to the Intelligence Section as a whole, since the General Staff also dealt with Operations and Training and had other abbreviations to denote these branches. The Intelligence Section was further subdivided and the part which dealt with Security was known as GSI(b). The junior Staff officers were graded as follows: Lieutenant-Colonel – first grade, Major – second grade and Captain – third grade, and were generally known as GSOs I, II and III. Thus I was normally identified in the Force Headquarters as the GSO III I(b).

I had been commissioned in the Indian Army in 1934 and appointed to the 9th Gurkha Rifles a year later. In 1939, having completed five years' service, I considered that I needed additional experience and accordingly applied for a Command Intelligence Course and was accepted.

I remember little of the course itself, except for one exercise in which the various syndicates had to proceed to the Headquarters town of one of the civil districts near Bareilly. In our case this was Budaun and we had to write a report on the Internal Security aspect of the District. The local authorities had been asked not to speak to us in English and as all the Magistrates and Police Officers were Indians, they obeyed their orders with gusto. However, we managed to get our information and I, as syndicate leader, duly prepared our report. I was interested and delighted to hear, years later, that it was still the 'standard' work on the district as late as 1946.

The result of this course was most encouraging; I was judged to be 'the best student' and recommended for a variety of army intelligence appointments. However, Civil Intelligence held a greater attraction for me and I was eventually offered an appointment as a Military Intelligence

Officer with the Civil Police. My Commanding Officer was extremely reluctant to let me go and this, plus the changed situation owing to the outbreak of war, caused him to refuse to allow me to accept this and other civil appointments offered.

My unit moved to the Khyber Pass in October 1939 and I continued at Regimental duty until one day in August 1940 when, without warning, I was placed on ten days' notice for service overseas in an appointment in the Field Security Police. None of my training at the Command Course had given me any idea of what the FSP, later to be called the Field Security Service or FSS, was supposed to do and Field Service Regulations were equally vague on the subject.

My then Commanding Officer, Ray Selby, reacted to this news by depriving me of any regimental appointments, on the very proper grounds that I was useless to him if I was not in a position to mobilise with the Battalion. I became an odd job man and so remained for over four months, as Army Headquarters kept me on notice until the end of December; then, without warning, I received a posting order to move to the Intelligence School which was to be formed in Karachi.

During the time that I was occupying myself as an odd job man, my Battalion took over a fort on the hills overlooking the Afghan border and I was sent there to act as temporary Commandant, in order to supervise the now relatively junior and inexperienced Company Commanders whose companies were in garrison. The name of this fort was Charbagh and the best description to give of it is to say that it was built of local stone, had galleries and loopholes and was, in fact, the counterpart of the forts made famous in the novels of P. C. Wren and further glorified in the films of those novels. My own bedroom had no window through which I could gaze upon the arid hills but had instead a heavy iron, loopholed shutter.

Intelligence to the lay mind implies action and excitement but at Charbagh I experienced its more normal aspect – drudgery and attention to detail in the hope that something

15

of use would eventually materialise; not for nothing do the French call this type of Intelligence the 'Service Statistique'. In the fort during the hours of daylight, two men of the Intelligence section were stationed to watch the Afghan military and customs post at Torkam which, by some quirk in the demarcation of the frontier, lay immediately below us. The fruits of this watching were sent each week to Army Headquarters at Delhi in the form of a log. In my time nothing of spectacular interest was recorded, the normal entries reading – 'Four Afghan soldiers came out' – 'Four Afghan soldiers went in' and similar variations of equal moment.

Now to return to Karachi. On arrival I found Major 'Jock' Campbell, the Commandant and a Captain 'Shackles' Majumdar and myself were to be Instructors Class C. Jock Campbell had Intelligence experience and had also been a Consul in Persia, Shackles had done a Command Course and had been an Air Liaison Officer, and I had no experience so, on the long accepted principle of 'the blind leading the blind', we started the School.

I instructed on two courses until, in the spring of 1941, I was rushed off to Iraq as a GSO III(I). My arrival in Basra preceded the outbreak of hostilities between the Iraq Army and ourselves by exactly one day. For the first few weeks I was the only Intelligence Officer in Force HQ, then things settled down and we acquired two more officers, both senior to me. Tony Boyce, who was to be the head of the Intelligence Branch as a GSO I, and the other, a regular officer of the British Service straight from the latest Quetta Staff College Course, who was destined for a second grade appointment. This gave us an experienced Head, a second grade staff officer who had qualified at the Staff College but who had had no Intelligence experience or training and a third grade officer, myself, with only a little Intelligence training. A discussion arose, not unnaturally, as to who would take the Operational section, I(a) and who the Security, I(b). Tony Boyce ruled that as Operational Intelligence required staff training, this should go to the GSO II and that as I had some Intelligence training, Security should be my responsibility; so fortuitous was my launching into Security Intelligence, a type of work in which I was to become deeply interested and also something of a pioneer in the Indian Army.

The Middle East Field Security Depot assisted us with British ranks and we were able to raise four 'Iraq Composite' Field Security Sections by the simple expedient of splitting two British and two Indian sections and joining the British and Indian halves into one Composite Section. These Composite Sections of one Officer, one Sergeant Major and six British ranks and one Jemadar and six Indian ranks subsequently formed the pattern for the raising of sections in Burma and later was adopted by the Depot in Karachi as standard practice for the Indian Army.

Luckily for us, the two British sections arrived from Cairo with very experienced Field Security Officers. This was a great blessing as none of our units had had any training in Security and most senior officers looked upon us as an unmitigated nuisance. However, by degrees, we gained the confidence of staff and units and gradually built up our organisation until, by the end of 1941, we had in addition to the Divisional Field Security Sections, static composite section in Basra, Shaiba and Baghdad and a fourth based on Baghdad, which occupied itself with railway security. I also managed to form a small 'Special Branch' of men with European language qualifications. These men did invaluable passport work on the land frontier between Syria and Turkey and, in particular, on the Taurus Express which ran twice weekly between Istanbul and Baghdad, and was one of the ways out of Axis occupied Europe.

In the early autumn of 1941, I was offered a month's leave in India but thinking that it was time I really learnt my job, I did a deal with the GSO I; if he would authorise me to take a month's tour with the 9th Army in Syria, with travel at Government expense, I would pay my own hotel bills and would work for fifty per cent of the time. He agreed to this and I travelled to Aleppo, by train through Turkey, as a civilian. From Aleppo I went on to Beirut and at the end of my month's 'leave', I returned by the same route. In Aleppo and Beirut, I contacted the local Field Security Officers and studied all aspects of their work, as well as making liaison visits to the Australian Corps Headquarters and Headquarters 9th Army. By the time I returned to Iraq, I felt that now I really knew something about Security work. However, my knowledge was not to be used in Iraq as, shortly after my return, I received the posting mentioned at the start of this book and which turned out to be that of GSO II I(b) Headquarters Burma Army.

It was one thing to receive a posting and be ordered out of Iraq but quite another to give effect to it. My presence being urgently required in Burma, I was to travel by air but, owing to the entry of Japan into the war, aircraft going East were few and far between and generally fully laden with essential personnel going either to Malaya or to the Dutch East Indies. Finally, in early January 1942, a seat was available in a civil KLM flight to Karachi.

On arrival at Karachi, I was met by 'Shackles' Majumdar who informed me that the Commandant of the Intelligence School, still Jock Campbell, requested that I should stop off there to lecture on the practical side of Security Intelligence. I was more than happy to accede to this request, after being assured that Army Headquarters would be notified of the reason for my delay. However, when I did arrive in Delhi, it transpired that the Intelligence School had omitted to notify Army Headquarters and I was told, with marked coldness, that my appointment had very nearly been given to another officer. I met my GSO I to be – Philip Gwyn, in Delhi. He was a down-to-earth Regular Officer of the 14th Punjab Regiment; an experienced Intelligence Officer who also had first-hand knowledge of the Japanese as he had been stationed in Shanghai, whilst qualifying as an Interpreter in Chinese. I had the privilege of serving under him both in the Burma Retreat and afterwards in Headquarters IV Corps

until the spring of 1943. No one could have had a better chief
– efficient, forthright and considerate.

In spite of Army Headquarters' displeasure at my tardy
arrival from Iraq, they were quite unable to move us to
Burma immediately. After about a week, we, that is Philip
Gwyn and myself, proceeded by Tata Air Lines to Calcutta
and thence in a DC2 of the Indian Air Force to Rangoon,
landing at Mingladon Airfield on 20 January.

In the First World War, Staff Officers were accused by the
front line troops, of living in luxury with every comfort provided; the Second World War emphasised that in this respect
too, times had changed. In the East it was customary to
travel with both your bedding and your servant and, until
now, the organisation of the Indian Army had taken this into
account. The advent of air travel, however, made this impossible and all the air passenger was allowed to take with
him was one suitcase.

The bombing of Rangoon, in December 1941, had caused
a panic and the flight of many of the servant class, with the
result that the principal hotel in Rangoon had closed and
although many servants did return, this hotel did not re-
open. There was nowhere therefore where a new arrival
could stay, except in an Army Mess and here one was expected to provide both a servant and bedding.

On the outbreak of hostilities Army Headquarters,
Burma, had taken over the main buildings of Rangoon University and its hostels. Philip Gwyn and I were duly taken to
one of these hostels, now an Army Mess and allocated
rooms. These rooms were furnished with beds but these, of
course, had no bedding on them nor even such an essential
item as a mosquito net. A reasonably good dinner was provided but the night that followed was decidedly uncomfort-
able and we welcomed the dawn.

After breakfast I went over to the Headquarters Offices –
located in the main building of the University – an imposing
three-storeyed building with verandas running round each
floor. At the gate were stationed one or two British ranks of

the Gloucestershire Regiment – Rangoon's garrison battalion. Their function was to ensure the security of the Headquarters but how they could do this since no one carried a pass, it was difficult to imagine. Identity Cards were, as yet, unknown in either India or Burma. The Intelligence Staff under the GSO I was divided into the conventional sections. The I(a) or Operational Intelligence was under the direction of an old friend of mine whom I had not seen for some years, 'Porky' Ewens of the Dorset Regiment. He had been a subaltern in the 1st Battalion when I served my post-Sandhurst attachment to them in 1934. A trained Intelligence Officer with a good knowledge of the Japanese Army and its methods, he had previously been on the Intelligence Staff in Malaya where he had acquired also a good knowledge of the neighbouring countries such as Thailand and French Indo-China. It was tragic that he should have died during the Retreat simply because there was no surgeon available to operate on him when he developed appendicitis. The I(b) or Security section was mine and my second-in-command, the GSO III, was Bill Talbot of the Queens Regiment. Bill was a war-time officer but in every way very typical of his Regiment, always smart and well turned out and very 'regimental' in his manner. He was a graduate of the Karachi Intelligence School but had had no practical experience.

The same could be said of Logan Gates, the GSO II of I(c) or the Press and Censorship section. He had little to do as there was little censorship, civil or military and the Public Relations Officers were rapidly absorbing the Press functions of I(c). In fact I(c) was abolished in the summer of 1942, its duties being divided between Public Relations and Censorship, both independent of the conventional Intelligence set up.

The final member of our team was the GSO II I(x) or Administration of Intelligence – Templar Widdicombe of my own Regiment and Battalion. He was of immense help to us as, although untrained in Intelligence, he was a staff Officer of Burma Army Headquarters of a year or more standing. This put him in the position of being able to advise us on the complicated and, to our minds, rather futile dovetailing of Army Headquarters' peace-time administrative and war-time operational functions. In particular, he was an expert in dealing with the bureaucratic methods of the Defence Department of the Government of Burma, which will be referred to in a later chapter.

My first priority was to acquire such necessaries as were essential to my well-being – bedding, a mosquito net, towels, etc., and last but by no means the least important, a servant. Templar was living in his pre-war bungalow and at this time still had his wife with him – her assistance was invaluable. Mrs Widdicombe was evacuated shortly afterwards. The first servant I acquired was a Madrassi Indian who had settled in Burma and married a Burmese wife. He was satisfactory in every way but, unfortunately, after a short time, in view of the deteriorating military situation, his wife persuaded him to remove himself to her village. However, before leaving he brought to me as his substitute, a young Madrassi boy and he remained with me until we finally reached India.

Security has been defined as the measures taken to prevent the enemy harming an Army by means other than those pertaining to the battlefield. The obvious methods are espionage, sabotage and propaganda. Fighting units, particularly when in the front line are security conscious of necessity. If they are not the enemy will infiltrate their positions and defeat them. Behind the lines things are very different and difficult. In addition to fighting units resting, there are vast depots of warlike stores, ammunition, food, petrol – everything that an Army needs for its very existence; there are the lines of communication – roads, railways and docks – all places where sabotage is relatively easy.

To combat these difficulties and disadvantages, an intensive programme of security education must be initiated to teach all units to be always on their guard and to trust no one. This requires an extensive coverage by Field Security

Sections working in the base areas and, of course, the provision of identity documents and passes to ensure physical security of vital installations. Our first task was to review our objectives and the forces available to carry them out. It was going to be extremely difficult to initiate these measures when the Japanese had already invaded Burma. For example, while it was possible to get Identity Cards printed, it was impossible for Officers of front line units to get photographs taken for these documents. It would not be untrue to say that except for the fact that the Japanese were already engaged with our units, Burma and its Army were still at peace.

We found that Burma had no Security personnel of her own. There was one Divisional FS section with the 17th Indian Division. The other Division, the 1st Burma, had none. The 17th Divisional section was an all Indian one, unlike our Composite Sections of British and Indian ranks which had proved successful in Iraq. It had been raised hastily and sent from the Depot at Karachi when the Headquarters of the Division had been ordered to Burma in late 1941. The Divisional Staff, having no idea of how to use their section, had attached it to the Divisional Employment Platoon, where it was carrying out general administrative duties. My immediate reaction was to get permission to remove this section to Rangoon, where it could be put to some use; at the same time the British NCOs of the Army HQ gate police were amalgamated to make our first Burma Composite Field Security Section. The Commanding Officer, Captain MacGilp, was an ex-employee of the Anglo-Iranian Oil Company and had been on field work. He had a tough, energetic manner and a full measure of sound common sense.

In the short time which remained before the military situation deteriorated to such an extent that we should have to make plans to continue our work in Northern Burma, the I(b) staff and our embryo Field Security Section busied themselves in organising security in Rangoon, overseeing the issue of identity cards, contacting the Police and the Civil Government Intelligence and Security organisations; in short, doing the hundred and one tasks necessary to build up a Security organisation in the Burma Army.

During this period which lasted approximately one month, we received some officer reinforcements from the Intelligence School at Karachi. We also acquired a jeep, probably one of the first to be used in the British forces. It was one of four donated by the Chinese authorities in charge of supplies landed at Rangoon en route to China. We had hardly begun to use this jeep when one of the young officers, a recent arrival, managed to turn it over. Luckily, it completed a full somersault and landed back on its wheels, with its engine still running and having sustained no damage other than a crushed windscreen. The occupants had been spilled out during the somersault but when I arrived shortly afterwards I found that none of them were seriously injured although all three officers were crestfallen and somewhat battered. My first question was, 'Is the jeep damaged?', and then I blasted all and sundry for their carelessness. On being asked later why I had expressed no sympathy for the injured I replied, 'I can get officers from Karachi but jeeps are irreplaceable.'

Amongst the new arrivals was Tony Sumersell, of the Seaforth Highlanders; he was keen to be a Field Security Officer and I arranged for him to be allotted to me. I also managed to secure two other officer volunteers for Field Security; Acomb, who had escaped from Laos and had been commissioned on his arrival in Burma, and Mansfield, an ex-regular British Warrant Officer of the Army Education Corps, who was bored with his office job in Ciphers.

I decided to keep MacGilp's new Composite FS Section with me in Rangoon and to 'back load' everyone else to Maymyo as soon as the military situation required a skeleton HQ to be set up there. Bill Talbot was to be in charge and he was to organise training courses for our new volunteers and organise them into sections.

23

II

Burma 1942 — Geography, People and Politics

To follow the story of the Burma Retreat, it is necessary to know something of the country as it was in 1942.

Burma, although small on the map when compared with her great neighbour India, is, in fact, a large country. Excluding the southernmost portion, it is roughly the same size as France, Belgium and Holland put together; that is, if one were to superimpose Burma on these countries, Rangoon would be on approximately the same latitude as Marseilles, Mandalay at Paris, Bhamo at Brussels and the northernmost tip well out into the North Sea. The north-west boundary with India would cut across Kent and Essex.

In addition to this land mass, there is a long finger stretching down and sharing the Isthmus of Kra with Siam. The southernmost tip is some 500 miles 'as the crow flies' from Rangoon and only some 300 miles from the northern border of Malaya. With the exception of the northern part around and to the east of Moulmein, which was the scene of the main Japanese attack, this area is not relevant to this book.

A characteristic of most parts of Burma is that the grain of the country runs north and south and this applies equally, therefore, to her rivers, railways and roads.

The two principal mountain ranges are like two fingers extended at an angle of roughly 30°. In the west and forming in its northern section, the boundary between Burma and India is a high range known from north to south as the Naga

24

Hills, the Chin Hills and the Arakan Yomas. In the Naga Hills the range rises to peaks of 12,000 ft and in the Chin Hills to between 8,000 and 10,000 ft. It is an area of tangled mountains and deep valleys, covered with dense jungle up to 6,000 ft and because of its rainfall, heat, insects and diseases it is probably one of the most difficult countries in the world in which to campaign. The Arakan Yomas are not as high as the Chin Hills but still form an effective barrier between Burma proper and the coastal strip to the north and south of Akyab.

In the east the mountain range, while equally high, is less unpleasant in all respects and has better communications. The range extends from the very north of Burma to the Isthmus of Kra. In these hills the frontier of Burma marches from north to south with that of China, of Indo-China where it reaches out to the Mekong River and of Siam in the south.

Lateral communication is made even more difficult because of a small range of hills known as the Pegu Yomas which divide the valley of the Irrawaddy from that of the Sittang.

Burma's greatest river, the Irrawaddy, and its tributary, the Chindwin, has always been both an asset and a bar to communication. In 1942 it proved to be a formidable obstacle as it was only bridged in one place – the great Ava Bridge near Mandalay, which carried both road and railway northwards over the Irrawaddy. On the other hand it was a great asset as it was navigable up to Myitkyina, some 1,000 miles from the sea and the Chindwin was navigable as far as Homalin, a slightly lesser distance. The British owned Irrawaddy Flotilla Company maintained regular passenger and goods services, and to many towns and villages the steamer was the only outlet. The Sittang, which is the central one of the three main rivers of Burma, rises near Meiktila and flows south through the central plain. The easternmost river, the Salween, rises in China and then flows south through the Shan States to enter the sea near Moulmein. Neither of these rivers is navigable. The Sittang, except near its mouth, was

BURMA

Scale 1:8,000,000

Railways

Roads

Tracks
motorabale in
dry season

Land over
3000 ft above
sea level

26

no great obstacle to movement and the Salween did not, except at Moulmein, influence the campaign.

The railways of Burma were of metre or 3 ft 3 in gauge and practically all single line. The main line from Rangoon ran north-eastwards to Pegu and then due north up the Sittang Valley to Mandalay. This line had a branch north-eastwards from Pyinmana to Kyaukpadang in the oilfield areas of the Irrawaddy Valley, and a lateral branch from Thazi, near Meiktila, to the escarpment of the Shan Hills near Taunggyi from where one of the few lateral roads ran east into the Shan States. A loop from Thazi through Myingyan rejoined the main line just south of Mandalay.

Mandalay itself was a terminus but, at a junction a few miles to the south, two important branches bifurcated. One paralleling the 'China' road, ran through the hills to Lashio. This line was a difficult one to work and guard as it involved a stiff climb with reversing stations in the forty odd miles between Mandalay and Maymyo, the summer capital, and then a long section of heavy engineering works, including the great Gokteik Viaduct, to Lashio. The other branch crossed the Irrawaddy by the Ava Bridge and ran to Myitkyina in the far north of the country, throwing off a short branch to Ye U, in the fertile plain of central Burma.

Another line ran north from Rangoon up the Irrawaddy Valley to Prome and there terminated; this had a lateral branch to Bassein in south-east Burma but this was interrupted by the unbridged Irrawaddy which had to be crossed by a railway ferry. To the south a branch ran from Pegu, across the Sittang River to Martaban, opposite Moulmein which lay across the Salween estuary and which again had to be crossed by ferry. From Moulmein a short section ran due south into Tennasserim. There was no connection between the Burma Railways and those of the neighbouring countries.

As might be expected in a country with a cheap and efficient river system of communication, plus a monopolistic State Railway, road communications had been neglected and were meagre in most areas. In fact, in the hilly areas of the Shan States, where there was neither river nor railway, roads were relatively more frequent. Lateral east to west roads were very infrequent and even the north to south trunk road system terminated at Mandalay. In general, there were little clusters of roads radiating from some river port or railway station but having no through communication with the rest of Burma.

The main trunk road was from Rangoon to Mandalay, via Pegu, following the railway and there was a secondary main road up the Irrawaddy Valley, through Prome, Magwe and oilfields near Yenangyaung but which also terminated at Mandalay. For the first 250 miles these two roads were separated by the Pegu Yomas and had no lateral connection whatsoever. A major road ran due east from Meiktila, through the Shan States, to the Indo-China border and a continuation of the main trunk road ran north-eastwards following the railway to Lashio and from thence on into China proper. This was the famous 'China' Road on which China depended for her supplies in her war with Japan and which was the only real road connection with the outside world.

In the south, a main road ran from Pegu to the Salween ferry at Martaban and in Tennasserim cart tracks went over the hills into Siam, notably at Kawkareik and farther south at the Three Pagodas Pass.

The ease of sea and river communications and the appalling difficulties of road building on and through the jungle clad mountains of the east meant that Eastern Burma was the worse off for roads. The whole of the coastal plain from Bassein, in the south, to Chittagong within India, in the north, was roadless except for the few feeders near a port. There was an indifferent road from the west bank of the Irrawaddy at Prome to Taungup but this terminated there and had no connection with any other roads. The only land communication with India was a poor cart track from Ye U in Central Burma to the Chindwin River near Kalewa, then a six-mile river trip to Kalewa, a short section of good road to Kalemyo and cart track again via Tamu to Palel, in the Indian State of Manipur. From Palel a good hill road ran to the rail head of Dimapur, in Assam, but connection onward to the Indian road system was by cart track. In view of the military necessity, work was in hand to improve this route but by early 1942 little had been accomplished.

Burma is inhabited by several races, the majority being the Burmans and the others the hill tribes of the perimeter hills. The Burmans, themselves, were intensely politically conscious and it must be remembered that the final conquest of Upper Burma, by the British, had taken place only some sixty years before, that is almost within living memory. As a result, there was a strong self-rule and anti-British party among the Burmans and dacoity (or banditry) was rife in many districts, either for political or private gain.

Of the hill peoples, the Shans were ruled by their local princes, the Sawbwas, very similar to the Indian Maharajas, and were not politically conscious. The hill tribes, the Chins, Kachins and Karens, were fiercely anti-Burman and as a result, pro-British and they remained so throughout the campaign. Of these the Karens were the most intelligent and although, originally, from the hills, had largely settled in the rice lands of Lower Burma. They were usually Christian by religion and at odds with their Buddhist Burman neighbours.

The various Burmese races were able to make a reasonable living under normal circumstances by rice cultivation and despised hard or dirty manual labour. This meant that the country was dependent for dock, railway and steamship labour on Indian coolies. The state of the country and its people was reflected in its armed services. The original Burma Rifles of the Indian Army was recruited entirely from the hill people but after the separation from India and a large degree of self-government in 1937, political pressure decreed the recruitment of Burmans. Many of the newer units were, therefore, of doubtful reliability particularly in the technical corps.

One very fine Corps did exist – the Burma Military Police

– who were used to police the frontier and tribal areas and to check dacoity in the interior. This force was under the Civil Government but organised on military lines with officers seconded from the Indian Army. It was recruited from the hill tribes but also contained a high percentage of Gurkhas, both from the Kingdom of Nepal and from those domiciled in Burma. On the separation from India this Corps was split into the Burma Frontier Force, to police the tribal areas and the Burma Military Police, to find the armed police for anti-dacoity operations and similar work in the interior districts. While the Corps was entirely loyal, the Burma Military Police did suffer from being disseminated throughout the country in small detachments and from a lack of training for war.

The climate of Burma is, in general, much like that of equivalent parts of India. In the coastal strips the weather is hot and humid throughout the year but elsewhere the months from October to March are pleasant, temperate and dry; from April to June it is hot and from June to September, when the monsoon is at its height, it is wet and humid. The rainfall in Central Burma is reasonable but it is extremely heavy in the coastal strips and over the hills, thus making any movement off a hard road almost impossible.

Burma was part of India, prior to April 1937, but the separation did not alter the type of government nor its various services. As in India, there had been a large degree of Burmanisation in the higher Civil Service appointments and in the higher ranks of the Police, amounting to not far off 50 per cent of the total. The lower officer ranks of the Civil Service and Police were entirely filled by those of Burmese nationality, although a fair proportion were, in fact, Anglo-Burmese or persons of mixed blood.

This large degree of self-government granted in 1937, continued until the autumn of 1941, when the Prime Minister was arrested for treasonable activities. The Governor, after prolonged negotiations with the politicians, managed to get an interim Ministry formed under Sir Paw Tun, one of the 'old guard' of Burmese politics. This dependence on a Ministry was one of the reasons for the great reluctance to proclaim any form of martial law or military rule, even in areas adjacent to the front line. Defence, however, was a 'reserved' subject for which the Governor, personally, and not the Ministry was responsible.

Burma maintained a Defence Department but to say that the Government of Burma, in 1942, was responsible for defence, was complete nonsense. It was true that prior to September 1939, Burma was responsible for and paid for her Defence forces but at that time the risk of invasion seemed small and the forces deemed necessary were in proportion to that risk. The outbreak of war and the attitude of Japan caused India to look upon Burma as an outlying bastion of her defences, and pressure was brought to bear on both Burma and the Chiefs of Staff in England to increase the forces available.

The Burmese politicians argued, with some justification, that the new risks were attributable solely to Burma's position in the general scheme of Imperial Defence and any forces additional to those required in 1939, should be paid for by England or India. This was accepted and so far as forces sent from India were concerned, little administrative bother occurred. It was otherwise with staff appointments or forces raised within Burma. Every such appointment required the formal sanction of the Government of Burma, even though no financial burden would fall on that country.

For example: I was appointed a GSO II in Headquarters Burma Army, by General Headquarters India, who were in operational command. The appointment had to be formally created by the Government of Burma, although my pay was the responsibility of the Government of India. This led to an exchange of letters in the style of 'I have the honour to state that a new appointment etc. etc.'. Queries and counter queries by the Defence Department followed before the final 'I have the honour to convey the sanction of the Governor of Burma etc.' letter was received. It was vital to recruit

British and Burmese ranks for our new Field Security Sections but before we could ask for volunteers, it was obvious that we ought to be able to notify them of the advantage of additional or Corps pay. We, in Burma, had no exact knowledge of what this was and as postal communication with India was by then almost non-existent, it was thought that a brief statement to the effect that British or Burmese Army ranks selected for Field Security Sections, would receive the same Corps pay as the equivalent British or Indian ranks employed in Indian Field Security Sections, should suffice. As this was the pay that these men would receive in due course and as the cost would be borne by India, this seemed a not unreasonable statement. The Defence Department, however, flatly refused to sanction it on the grounds that that could not be committed to anything of which they had no precise knowledge. Much futile and time-consuming correspondence accrued before the matter was resolved.

In the interests of justice it must be said that I always found the various officers of the Defence Department most friendly and helpful but they were committed to a bureaucratic procedure which seemed nonsensical in the middle of a campaign and at a time when the Japanese were not only on Burmese soil but actually at the gates of Rangoon.

III

The Evacuation of Rangoon — Early Days

Before continuing the story, it is necessary to go back a little, and give a brief resumé of the forces available to repel a Japanese invasion and to elucidate how these forces fared during the period after my arrival in Burma on 20th January until the evacuation of Rangoon, which started on 20th February, just one month later.

The General Officer Commanding-in-Chief in Burma was Lieutenant-General T. J. Hutton. He had been appointed to this post in the previous December, having been specially selected by General Sir Archibald Wavell, the Commander-in-Chief in India, for his drive and administrative ability. He had held the appointment of Chief of the General Staff in India prior to this. The senior officer with whom I had most dealings was General Hutton's principal staff officer – the Brigadier General Staff – Brigadier Davies.

By the time that General Hutton arrived, the forces in Burma consisted of the 1st Burma Division of the 1st and 2nd Burma Brigades and two Indian Brigades, the 13th and 16th. General Hutton had appreciated that Tennasserim could not be held and that the most likely routes for an invasion would be either through the north of Tennasserim and directed on Moulmein or into the Southern Shan States. To counter this threat, two brigades were located in the Shan States, one brigade with additional troops in Moulmein and the reserve brigade at Mandalay. There were two British battalions in Burma, mainly for internal security duties and of these, the 2nd Battalion Kings Own Yorkshire Light Infantry (KOYLI) was placed in the 1st Burma Brigade and the other, the 1st Battalion Gloucestershire Regiment was the garrison battalion of Rangoon.

On 9th January, the Headquarters of the 17th Indian Division, commanded by Major-General J. G. Smyth, VC, arrived in Rangoon and was placed in command of the forces in the Moulmein area; these consisted of the original garrison of the 2nd Burma Brigade, the 16th Indian Brigade from Mandalay and the 46th Indian Brigade, newly arrived from India.

At the same time the Generalissimo Chiang Kai-shek offered the Vth and VIth Chinese Armies to help defend Burma. These were each the size of a British Division and did not arrive in Burma, in any strength, until after the fall of Rangoon.

Various reinforcements, including a complete Australian Division, were promised at various times, but the only additional fighting troops actually to arrive were the 7th Armoured Brigade, comprising two Regiments of light tanks from the Middle East, two Indian brigades, the 48th and 63rd, and three or four unbrigaded British Infantry Battalions from Internal Security garrison duties in India.

It must be realised that with the exception of the 7th Armoured Brigade, which had seen service in the Middle East, and the 48th Indian Brigade, which consisted of three regular Gurkha Battalions of very high morale and a fair standard of training, the troops of the Burma Army were generally in no condition to meet a cunning, well trained and ruthless enemy. The various Indian brigades came from different Indian divisions in training in India, which had been ruthlessly broken up to provide piecemeal reinforcements for Malaya and Burma; the battalions themselves were either regular battalions which had been severely 'milked' to provide the nucleus of new battalions or newly raised battalions. Both categories were sadly deficient in experienced officers and NCOs. Few battalions had had much practical training in their present brigades and in some cases had come direct from service in the North West Frontier. None had been trained under jungle conditions. The British battalions, both in Burma and from India had done nothing but garrison duties since war broke out and were soft in the extreme. The inevitable result was that there was little mutual trust within formations or by formations in one another; commanders did not know their units nor officers their men. Conditions were such that it was impossible to withdraw complete brigades from the line for rest or re-equipping and therefore, each time a disaster occurred the same brigades were hastily re-constituted with units from another sector. This effectively stopped any continuity within formations.

The fighting units, considering their training and experience, did better than might have been expected but, not unnaturally, morale was not always of the highest and discipline sometimes failed, both individually and in certain units. There were times behind the lines when the situation came near to getting out of hand and the administrative units close to becoming a rabble. The complete absence of any units of the Corps of Military Police, British or Indian, did not help and as will be seen in later chapters, there were times when the only units capable of undertaking their tasks were the Field Security Sections.

It is hardly surprising that the one month between 20th January and 20th February saw a series of disasters. Briefly, the Japanese attacked on the border on 20th January and by 31st January they had captured Moulmein. They then crossed the Salween on the 9th February and arrived at the Bilin River by 16th February and had forced the British forces back from their positions there by about the 20th February. 17th Indian Division then started withdrawing to the Sittang River line and preparations were made to blow the combined road and railway bridge. Unfortunately, the Japanese pushed on so fast that they arrived at the bridge before the greater part of the 17th Indian Division had reached it. The bridge had to be blown when over half the Division were still on the wrong side and of those who did manage to get away, all did so by swimming across. This resulted in units losing all cohesion and by the time they arrived at Pegu, the Division had ceased to exist as a fighting formation. Only 80 officers and 3,400 other ranks were left and of these only about 1,500 had their rifles. However, the Division was re-equipped at Pegu and made a remarkable recovery.

This disaster effectively put an end to any idea of defending the Sittang line and it was only a matter of time before the Japanese would improvise means of crossing the river. They had forced the front door of Burma proper and could now move south-west to Rangoon or north up the main road towards Mandalay. To counter this threat 17th Indian Division, or what was left of it, remained at Pegu in order to prevent a move on Rangoon and the 1st Burma Division handed over the defence of the Southern Shan States to the Chinese VIth Army and moved to block an enemy movement northward up the main road and railway.

Now to return to events in Rangoon. During the early part of my time there things were reasonably normal. There had been a big exodus of labour after the December air raids but many had returned, encouraged by the cessation of such raids. Shops were open, clubs and restaurants functioning and public transport working. As the Japanese came nearer, things slowly deteriorated. It was quite a slow process and was geared to a general rundown of the capital. Government Departments began to move out, static military installations were sent north and private businesses began to close down. Few officers at Army Headquarters during this period thought that there would be much chance of holding Rangoon. This was no defeatist attitude but a realisation that without massive reinforcements of men and materials all that could be done was to hold the Japanese off the Indian border by a long and slow retreat.

The Official History details various moves, conferences and so on between the various senior Commanders and the British Government as to whether or not Rangoon should be held as Tobruk had been and indeed, the later replacement of General Hutton by General Alexander was intended to be a step in this direction. Naturally, all this went over the heads of those of us who were in comparatively junior positions. During the later developments in Rangoon we merely carried out our orders on a day-to-day basis.

By the 20th February, things had deteriorated to such an extent that General Hutton ordered the first phase of the evacuation, known as the 'E' Label. This was so called because windscreen labels with the letter 'E' were issued and after this date any vehicle found in Rangoon without such a label would be requisitioned or immobilised and the labels were only issued to those whose presence was deemed to be essential. This proclamation did not mean an immediate or massive exodus; Rangoon had been dying for the last two weeks and many had already left. It did mean that steps had to be taken immediately to provide means of evacuation for all who now wished to leave, and to move the remaining personnel of Government Departments and semi-official agencies, such as Port Trust, municipal and hospital staffs, police and jail personnel. To prevent these people leaving before it was absolutely necessary, they had all been given a promise that they would be evacuated in good time. The only practical way out was by rail, either direct to Mandalay by the main line, now dangerously close to the front line, or by the subsidiary line to Prome, from where refugees would have to proceed onward by road by whatever means they could contrive.

The 'E' label had hardly been announced when I was told to take such Field Security personnel as I had in Rangoon, to help the railway authorities with the evacuation. This was MacGilp's Section, afterwards to become No. 1 Burma FS Section. The Burma Railways, in normal circumstances, were an efficient concern but had the usual shortcomings inherent in railways in non-industrialised countries in the East. With the exception of the suburban lines around Rangoon, much of the main and all of the branch lines were single track with crossing stations at about ten-mile intervals. The safe working of trains at any reasonable frequency depended, therefore, on staff being in each of the crossing stations to work the block token apparatus. As has been said earlier, the Burmese did not take kindly to work of a heavy, manual nature and this meant that outside of the clerical grades and to a certain extent, the station masters and guards, few Burmese were to be found. The place of local races was taken by the Anglo-Burmese or Indians for drivers and firemen and by Indians of the coolie class in the lower grades. There were also a large number of Indians in the traffic grades, in particular, the Assistant Station Masters on whom the signalling of the trains in the intermediate stations depended. In the weeks immediately preceding the 'E' label day, the Indian staff had been gradually slipping away – particularly from the Rangoon and Pegu areas. In an effort to hold the staff and to give the senior railway officers more authority, the remaining staff were militarised and a senior railway officer, Lieutenant-Colonel Brewitt, was appointed Deputy Director of Railways in the Rangoon area, and it was to him I reported for orders.

MacGilp had managed to get a requisitioned house in the residential area, not far from the railway station and had established his section in it. I moved in with him, but took most of my meals with the railway officers who had set up a 'mess' in the Railway Administration building. By this time, we were beginning to look scruffy; the lack of a dhobi (Indian washerman) meant that even if one could get one's shirts and shorts washed, they could not be ironed. Our personal arms were very varied; the Indian ranks of MacGilp's Section had .38 pistols in webbing holsters but most of the British ranks had no arms at all, their units having retained them. These men we armed with various weapons, mostly police riot guns – 'pump' action single-barrelled shotguns which could fire anything from a 'lethal bullet' to No. 8 shot. We found small shot very useful later on when dealing with looters. Probably the most useful weapon, at this time, were a number of police 'lathis', the six foot bamboo staves tipped at both ends with brass. My personal arms consisted of a German Walther Automatic, still bearing the insignia of the Persian Police as it had been issued to me in Baghdad in exchange for my .45 revolver, as these weapons were urgently needed by the forward troops, and a lathi. All in all, we looked like a band of revolutionary cut-throats than soldiers of the King.

The Railway's plan for the evacuation was to run one train daily direct to Mandalay, for the so-called 'privileged evacuees', those who had been guaranteed a safe passage out of Rangoon, and a shuttle service to Prome for the rest. The shuttle service gave little trouble other than the shortage of staff, as the line was going away from the front line and was reasonably secure from enemy attention. The Mandalay train, which was supposed to run on the timings of the daily train 'No. 1 Up-Mail', or as near to them as possible, was a very different story. The line ran through Pegu and as a result of the Sittang Disaster was, for a considerable distance on both sides of that town, very close to the Japanese with a distinct possibility that they might infiltrate our forces and cut the line. There were no staff at all in any station between Rangoon and Pegu, resulting in no block system of signalling being operative nor was the line patrolled by the usual permanent way gangs. Luckily, the line was double and so the possibility of collision was small. Our normal method of working was to telephone Pegu to find out if any train already dispatched had arrived and provided it had, launch another 'into the blue' with no knowledge of how it was faring until it arrived at Pegu. The farther north a train went, the easier things became as more stations were manned and by about Toungoo things were normal, relatively speaking.

In addition to these trains, the Railway Administration

was still trying to run a public service of sorts in central and northern Burma, troop specials to move the 1st Burma Division from the Shan States to the Upper Sittang Valley and supply trains from the new Depots established in the Mandalay–Shwebo area. In the Rangoon district, although the back loading of munitions and stores northward had ceased, supply trains were still required for the 17th Indian Division at Pegu and, in addition, the 63rd Indian Brigade had to be moved later from Rangoon to Pegu.

Rangoon Station was a through station, the line to the west proceeding to Prome and that to the east to Pegu. It had four platforms connected by a footbridge from the main entrance and offices on the north side. It was well fenced, being in the centre of the city, an unusual thing for stations in the East and this made our task of crowd control much easier.

All the subordinate staff had decamped and all that remained was a handful of railway officers, mostly British but including one young Burmese Assistant Traffic Superintendent, a few Anglo-Burmese traffic staff and guards and a fair number of Anglo-Burmese drivers and firemen. The main staff problem was the complete absence of the Indian coal coolies and the result was that the already overworked engine crews had to coal their own engines. On several occasions we had a train loaded and ready to go in every respect except that it lacked an engine. We could get no reply, by telephone, from the Engine Shed as all the staff were out in the yard preparing engines. Finally, a messenger had to be sent on foot to the Shed, a mile or so down the line.

The Prome trains were not a great problem, as I have said earlier, and there was no restriction on who could use them and our main concern was to keep order, prevent dangerous overcrowding and see that the trains were filled with people rather than luggage; a strict rule of one package per person had to be enforced. Many tried to move their entire household effects or their stock in trade and heart rending appeals were made to us that the abandonment of these goods would mean financial ruin but we had to be adamant. Had we been dishonest, we could have made our fortunes for bribes were offered freely. Our task at the station could be summarised: to oversee the general security of the area, to ensure that the trains were loaded in an orderly manner and to prevent riot and last but not least, to protect the railway staff from interference or attack.

'The 'privileged evacuees' train, No. 1 Up-Mail, was a real headache. It ran straight through to Mandalay and therefore everyone wanted to get on board, whether they had any right there or not. The persons entitled to travel were a very mixed bunch, extending through every stratum of society from Government clerical and subordinate officers to coolies and hospital sweepers, the latter categories prone to panic and without discipline.

Colonel Brewitt asked me to take over the loading of this train, merely giving me each day a list of the Departments entitled to travel and a rough estimate of the respective numbers involved. The train was due to depart at about 3 p.m. but by noon the station forecourt was a seething mass of humanity and baggage. There was no public address system and so we had to make the best use we could of a megaphone. The first essential was to call inside the station, the senior official of each party and check with him the exact number of travellers. He was then told to return to his party, explain to them that places would be found for all and impress upon them the need to behave quietly and not on any account to panic. The official concerned was ordered to report back at about 1 p.m. accompanied by a reliable man who would act as a guide. One of the main deterrents to breaking the rules was the fear that the culprit would forfeit his place on the train and it was this fear which did most to ensure orderly behaviour.

As soon as the train drew up at the platform, I, personally, allotted the accommodation, marking the compartment doors in chalk with the name of the party. The leaders and guides were brought to the entrance gate when loading commenced and the leader of the first party to load stood by the gate through which the evacuees had to pass in single file; he was supported by two Field Security men with lathis at the ready. The respective leaders had been warned that they must personally identify each member of their party as they passed through the gate. The gate was then opened and the evacuees were allowed to pass in and were led to the train by the guides. Anyone trying to gatecrash or legitimate travellers with more than one package got a good whack from a lathi and were pushed away from the gate. The legitimate traveller was allowed back when he had divested himself of his surplus baggage. Loading was also a problem as we were putting considerably more into the carriages than they were designed to hold. A metre gauge 3rd class carriage was designed to seat about 80 persons but we were cramming in at least one hundred people. All available space was utilised – lavatories, luggage vans and guards vans, except for one reserved for the guard himself. On the whole, except for the noise which was greatly in excess of the hubbub normally to be heard in a busy Eastern station, the loading was orderly enough although every now and then there were disputes or even fights which had to be quelled. I recall one incident of a man so panic-stricken that he had lost all sense of reason and was even trampling on other people in his anxiety to get into the train. He was completely deaf to any appeals and as panic is infectious, I hit him smartly on the head with my lathi and he collapsed but before we had time to attend to him, he staggered to his feet and proceeded quietly but shakily to the train.

On the second day of the evacuation a nasty and what might well have developed into a very serious incident occurred. A large proportion of the rank and file of the Rangoon City Police were not Burmese but Indians, mostly Sikhs and Punjabi Mussulmans; police in the East are seldom popular with the public and where they are of an alien race, often hated. The Police had become very jumpy therefore; at the back of their minds they had the fear that should they fall into Japanese hands, they would be handed over to the mob. There was a strong rumour that this had happened when Tavoy in Tennasserim had been occupied and the police had remained at their posts. I was allotting accommodation in the train when I was told that a body of well over a hundred police in uniforms – all Indians – were congregated in the station forecourt and threatening to storm the barrier. On arrival there, I found about four or five Field Security ranks – British and Indian – facing a mob which was completely out of hand. No appeals by megaphone were of any avail so the only thing to do was to draw up the few men I had, with their arms at the ready, and warn the Police that as soon as the first man tried to storm the barrier, we should open fire on them. This threat seemed to have little or no effect but the situation was saved by the arrival of the Deputy Commissioner of Police, Mr Bestall, who had come to make arrangements for the transport of these men to Prome. He grabbed the megaphone and the sound of his voice, well known to them, calmed his men. He told them that he was thoroughly ashamed of them; they had been guaranteed a passage to Prome and this would be honoured. Finally he told them that they would be handed over to me and impressed upon them that any man who disobeyed my orders would certainly not be put on the train and would stand a good chance of being shot.

After the departure of the Mail train we set about loading the Police into a train for Prome. They were orderly enough but it now transpired that on their way to the station they had systematically looted the cloth market. Every man had at least one bundle of brand new bolts of cloth, sheets, towels, etc., as well as his personal kit. In the altercations which followed, some of my Field Security, particularly the Indian ranks, gave any policeman who was slow to relinquish his bundle of loot a good beating with their lathis. In the middle of this fracas, the Commissioner, Mr Prescott, arrived in a furious rage and demanded to know why the Field Security were beating the Police. I replied hotly, regardless of his high rank, that I should like to know why he had sent the Police up to the station without prior warning, why they had become a disorderly mob and why had they looted the cloth market. I then added, for good measure, that he should be thankful that I had not opened fire on them. This incident caused a coldness between us which lasted for the duration of the evacuation.

The only other incident of note was an altercation with an American airman of the Chinese-American Volunteer Group (AVG). He turned up demanding train space for his Anglo-Burmese girl friend and got into an argument with a Sikh Naik of the Field Security and in a fit of temper he pulled the Sikh's beard. The Sikhs are a proud race and to pull their beards is a great insult; the Naik was so insensed that he was threatening to shoot the American then and there. Fortunately for the American, I was able to get hold of the Jemadar of the Field Security who relieved the Naik and sent him back to his quarters to cool off and the American was advised to push off and not to come back again.

Before concluding the story of the railway evacuation, I must give the highest praise to the railway men remaining on duty and in particular to the Anglo-Burmese drivers and firemen. It takes great courage to take out a train towards the enemy lines without any escort and it took even greater courage to bring back your locomotive and empty train for another load when once you have reached comparative safety. The work of the RAF and AVG also deserves great praise. We were spared air raids which would have made our tasks quite impossible, thanks to their seeing off the Japanese before they could attain their targets.

After about five days things were quiet enough at the station to leave matters in the hands of MacGilp and his section. I reported back to Army Headquarters or rather to the skeleton of it which still remained in Rangoon, expecting that I should be told to move off to Maymyo in order to rejoin my echelon which had already gone there, but my orders were not as I had expected – Rangoon and its problems were to occupy me for a while yet.

IV

The Evacuation of Rangoon — Last Days

'You have sold me out to the Army!' This intriguing statement was being shouted on the stairs of Army Headquarters as I was going up to report to Philip Gwyn. The two men coming down were Prescott, the Commissioner of Police, who was the one shouting and Phelips, the Secretary of the Defence Department, who was endeavouring to pacify him.

I continued on my way, little realising that this altercation was to have a direct bearing on my future. I was expecting to leave Rangoon shortly and to join up with the remainder of the Intelligence Staff in Maymyo but a surprise awaited me, for on entering Philip Gwyn's office he said, 'You have got to get back to the city and take charge of Law and Order, Churchill has ordered that Rangoon be held and we have got to bring in a complete Australian Division through the docks.' This was a complete reversal of what I had always thought our policy to be – that of a slow withdrawal towards the Indian border, with no special significance being placed on Rangoon.

Detailed orders and explanations followed and I learnt also that General Hutton was being superseded by General Alexander, at that time known as the 'last ditcher' of Dunkirk. It appeared that Churchill was so impressed by the resistance of Tobruk that we were to do the same. Unfortunately, there were great differences between the two places, the main one was that although we had temporary mastery in the air, we had not command of the sea. Further, Rangoon, although a great port was not physically 'on the sea' and shipping had to approach by many miles of narrow waterway which could be commanded by land artillery. Finally, the troops provided for the defence, if they all materialised, were woefully inadequate – an Australian Division newly arrived from the Middle East, the remnants of the 17th Indian Division at about half strength and still recovering from the Sittang disaster, a newly formed and untried Indian Brigade, the 63rd, and the 1st Field Regiment Indian Artillery also without any battle experience. Luckily for the Australian Division it was diverted by its own Government for the defence of its homeland and this meant that no defence of Rangoon could possibly succeed.

However, this is anticipating events; the immediate task was to provide a suitable climate in which to bring a considerable body of troops over the docks and through the city. Civil authority had ceased to exist although a small number of police still remained. The jails had been emptied by the simple expedient of releasing the prisoners and the same measures were taken at the lunatic asylum. This meant that a number of dangerous criminals and lunatics were abroad and they celebrated their freedom by looting, burning and fighting each other. It was essential to keep certain services going in the city – power, light, telephones, dock services and in the absence of specialised Army units, all these had to be done by civilians, Europeans or Anglo-Burmese. These people were, in the main, unarmed and living in their own homes. The chief requirement, therefore, was to make the city reasonably safe for them to go about their normal duties.

The new plan made the Commanding Officer of the Gloucestershire Regiment, whose troops were garrisoning Rangoon, the Military Governor and I was appointed Assistant Military Governor in charge of law and order. The Military Governor was to ensure the security of the city from enemy infiltration or parachutists and I was to control all forces directly engaged in the maintenance of law and order but under the Military Governor's general direction.

The actual verbal orders which I received were that Rangoon would be put under 'military control', in view of the breakdown of civil authority. No mention of martial law was ever made and the only reference to this take over, in the Official History, is 'the imposition of a curfew and orders to military patrols and such police as remained, to shoot looters on sight stopped the worst of the looting'. In actual fact, no curfew as such was ever imposed; this was rendered unnecessary as all the usual inhabitants had left and anyone remaining was either in the Services, an essential civilian or an undesirable. Later we devised various means of dealing with the latter and these had the added advantages of being more humane and of some use to ourselves.

The title of Military Governor was not perpetuated as the Governor of Burma, Sir Reginald Dorman-Smith, objected to it as derogatory to his authority and it was altered to Military Commandant. This sort of quibble in no way altered our responsibilities and my task remained that of an Assistant Military Governor of a city which was without civilian government.

On receiving my orders, I went straight to Police Headquarters in Mogul Street, commonly called 'the Mogul Guard', to take stock of the available forces. As far as the regular police were concerned, there were five gazetted (commissioned) officers; the Commissioner – Prescott, the Deputy Commissioner – Bestall, the Superintendent of Port Police, and two Assistant Commissioners. There were also about forty-five Sergeants, a rank restricted to Europeans and Anglo-Burmese and ranking roughly with an Inspector. Of the Indian and Burmese Inspectors and Constables, none were present. My own resources were MacGilp's FS Section, six or seven British ranks, the same number of Indian ranks and one or two Burmese. I had been promised some detachments of the Burma Military Police to act as static guards and these were of great use in securing the 'Mogul

Guard', the power station, the telephone exchange and other essential buildings.

I reported to the Commissioner and his welcome was cold in the extreme. His theme was 'you have superseded me, it's your responsibility, now get on with it'. I have often wondered why, if he felt so strongly, he did not resign and go. However, by the time the final evacuation came our relations were better and I came to sympathise with his position. To have seen his proud and efficient force disintegrate before his eyes must have been a very embittering experience. Bestall and the other officers were quite prepared to take my orders, and they gave me much valuable advice. They advised me that the best way to stop the looting was to drive the looters out of the main market, where they were in almost crowd proportions.

This market was within a stone's throw of the Mogul Guard so we mustered a force of police and Field Security men and on arrival ordered the looters to disperse. They paid no heed. We had no option but to open fire on them and drive them straight out of the market; regrettably some four or five were killed and a number wounded but as they were taken away later, by their compatriots, it is not known whether any of the wounded succumbed to their injuries. The decision to fire on the crowd was a very unpleasant one to take but, in the circumstances, it was the lesser of two evils. News of our action must have spread rapidly amongst the criminal elements because mob looting never occurred again, only isolated instances. Arson was another serious problem and one which we never really mastered, with the result that large portions of the city were burnt out.

One of my orders was to secure all liquor on or near the docks, as we were expecting a considerable body of troops to arrive by sea during the course of the next few days. These stocks varied from 'Chinese spirit' to excellent whisky, gin and brandy, and they were mostly in bonded stores on the docks. The casks of 'Chinese spirit' were staved in and the contents poured into the harbour; the fumes from this stuff were so strong that one felt giddy merely from inhaling them. The whisky, gin and brandy presented a problem as everyone was extremely loath to destroy it. The representative of the Rangoon Branch of the Reserve Bank of India suggested it be placed in the Bank vaults and this was duly done. The currency notes normally kept there had either been evacuated to India or burnt and I have often wondered what the Japanese reactions were when they eventually got into the vaults and found no currency but only alcohol. No doubt their firm convictions about the degeneracy of the British were amply confirmed.

Corpses posed a great problem, particularly as a number of them were on the docks and the climate did nothing to lessen the problem. It was never determined how they came to be there but we thought that the most likely explanation was that there had been a battle between rival gangs of criminals over the possession of loot. Corpse disposal and similar types of work, in the East, is done only by the sweeper class and they had all left Rangoon. It would have been unthinkable to order the Indian ranks to do such work and this left only the British ranks of the Field Security. I was forcibly reminded, while clearing the dock area, of the expression 'dead weight'. We were endeavouring to push a corpse which had obviously been there too long, into the water; we used long poles to push with and it took the concerted efforts of five of us before we could finally accomplish our end. Later on we got better organised and formed a 'corpse squad', consisting of two British ranks with a small police van, smothered in disinfectant, to act as hearse and the 'undertaker's' men were provided from among looters caught 'flagrante delicto' and this was one of our improvised punishments.

In taking stock of the situation in Rangoon and the activities of the 'last ditchers', it is interesting to note how much was still functioning. We had made the main part of the city reasonably safe for ordinary people and cleared it of corpses, many of which constituted a grave risk to health; the power station was working and continued to supply us with light and power until the afternoon of the last day. The same can be said of the compressor station which kept the sewage flowing, and, thanks to the English Chief Engineer of the Rangoon Corporation, we were still able to get drinking water. Rangoon had three main telephone exchanges, all manual, of which two belonged to the private Telephone Company and the third was the Government exchange. We could get all numbers on the latter and a selection of key numbers on the private exchanges. There was one volunteer Auxiliary Fire Service Team and detachments from the Port Trust and Railways.

It was not long after my appointment that we heard that the Australian Division was not going to arrive but in spite of this we had to continue our work as the 63rd Indian Brigade and the 1st Indian Field Regiment still had to be brought in. Now that mass looting had ceased, although we had been given full discretionary power to shoot looters on sight, this seemed to be an unnecessarily brutal way of dealing with them. We were hampered by the complete absence of the mechanics for criminal proceedings; there were no magistrates, courts, or even prisons, so we opened the police 'lock-up' as a makeshift. It was normally used for short periods of incarceration for prisoners awaiting trial and had three or four large cells capable of holding some twenty to thirty persons, each cell had a water-tap and an Indian type latrine. Our prisoners had to be turned loose within 24 hours as we had no way of feeding them, so each morning we held a 'general jail delivery' – selected the 'corpse squad' who would be set free after work and gave the remainder six of the best with a bamboo before letting them go.

I still do not know under what laws or authority we acted but I am certain that our methods were at least humane and, right or wrong, they worked for within the centre of the city complete calm prevailed. This was not so in the suburbs and an amusing incident occurred which had repercussions later. A report was received that a gang of local Chinese were loot-

ing a godown (storehouse) attached to a house in the suburbs. On arrival we found that this godown contained a fair
number of cases of beer. At first I was at a loss as to how to
dispose of it but then inspiration came to me – the fighting
troops had had few comforts of late so why should not the
contents of this godown provide them with some? I, therefore, took two or three cases for the Field Security, gave a
few more to the police and had the remainder removed to
the Supply Depot, telling the Supply Officer to issue it free
to units as and when they came in for their rations.

The story must have got around as, about a year later, I
was asked by the Government of Burma in Exile whether I
had requisitioned the beer, as the owners were pressing for
payment. I replied, briefly, that the beer had been abandoned
and I had only put it to good use. This was not the only
commodity I was thought to have requisitioned – coal and
rice were included.

No facilities existed for buying anything in the normal
way and this proved to be an added hardship to units of the
17th Indian Division who had lost everything in the crossing
of the Sittang and especially to the Officers' Messes which
had no cutlery or crockery. It should perhaps be mentioned
why the Officers were harder hit than their men. In large
areas of the East it is more normal to use one's right hand
for conveying food to the mouth than to use a spoon or fork
so the Indian troops were less inconvenienced in this respect.

We instituted a system of 'permits to loot' to cope with the
situation and this rather odd procedure was brought about as
a result of the following incident. A report was received that
Rangoon's largest department store was being looted. We
raced there in a jeep and burst into the main part of the
building and saw, at the end of a long sales gallery, an Indian
soldier with a huge pile of boxes. I was in the lead and let
fly with a charge of No. 8s from my riot gun; the soldier
let out a yell, dropped the boxes and bolted with us in pursuit. On turning a corner we ran into a Lieutenant-Colonel
who barked out in fury: 'What the hell do you mean by

shooting at my man?' I replied with equal heat, 'What do you mean by looting? Do you know that I can take you out and shoot you out of hand?' This elicited an unexpected and plaintive reply. 'It's a bit hard – we do the fighting – lose everything we've got and when we come in here to buy what we need, we can't and get threatened with being shot into the bargain.' Needless to say, no further obstacles were put in his way.

It was this episode which led me to discuss the problem with the Military Governor and he saw the wisdom of issuing instructions for the provision of 'permits to loot'. Anyone, in a situation similar to that of the Colonel, could apply to the Station Staff Officer at Sale Barracks, Rangoon, and, if considered to be a genuine case he was given a permit to collect certain types of article, mostly for Mess use, to replace those lost by enemy action. The recipient then brought the permit to the Mogul Guard where someone was deputed to go with him to collect the necessary items.

I, myself, had to loot a watch and this was a source of amusement to my colleagues for a long time. It happened quite early on that my own wristwatch strap broke and my watch falling on to the hard concrete of the station platform, broke into its component parts. A watch being an essential, I went round every jewellers' shop, only to be confronted by empty show cases, but at last I found a small lady's watch on a thin black ribbon and promptly looted it; from then on and right up to the end of the retreat, I was teased and questioned about the Burmese girl I was assumed to have taken it from, where was she and what had I done with her and other similar witticisms.

The days passed; 63rd Indian Brigade came in but still there was uncertainty as to our future. No decision could be made until the arrival of General Alexander and he did not reach Rangoon until 5th March, and even at that late hour he was not prepared to yield Rangoon without first trying to restore the situation on the Pegu front. The inevitable result was another near disaster for 17th Indian Division and the loss of Pegu, with the Japanese now between this Division and 1st Burma Division near Toungoo.

It would be unfair to blame this situation on General Alexander; he had been subjected to political pressures in London and, in fact, he had been appointed with the object of holding Rangoon. He had been briefed by Wavell as late as 3rd March and he, according to the Official History, had seriously under-estimated the Japanese strengths and over-estimated the power and capacity of the British Indian forces. Little of this was known to us at the time, for we were fully occupied with our routine tasks of policing Rangoon but it did bring us to within a hair's breadth of becoming inmates of a Japanese prison camp.

Our daylight hours were relatively quiet during the last days but not so the nights. We could never completely master the problem of arson for, with our meagre resources, we could only deal with vital areas in the centre of the city. Several nights were spent by the Police and Field Security in helping the Auxiliary Fire Service team, instead of enjoying a quiet sleep in their beds. On one particular night a building very close to the Mogul Guard was ignited and we were hard pressed to prevent the fire spreading to our Headquarters. I well remember standing on the roof of the burning building at about 2 a.m. engaged in throwing down hot tiles, to lessen the risk of further combustion. On another night, a Gloucestershire Regiment patrol in an armoured car, turned into Mogul Street and not hearing the challenge of a Gurkha post of the Burma Military Police, engaged in a shooting match; one Gurkha was injured before we could stop the skirmish.

In view of the turn of events were obviously taking, I consulted the Military Governor about the position of the Field Security and myself should a final evacuation be ordered and received the heartening news that we should be evacuated with the remaining Police, by sea. This gave a good boost to our morale, but 'the best laid schemes o' mice and an' men gang aft a-gley', and so it was in this instance.

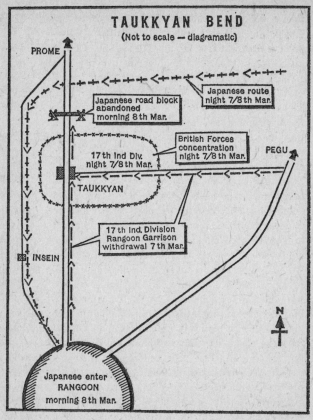

TAUKKYAN BEND

(Not to scale — diagramatic)

PROME

Japanese route
night 7/8th Mar.

Japanese road block
abandoned
morning 8th Mar.

British Forces
concentration
night 7/8th Mar.

17th Ind Div.
night 7/8th Mar.

PEGU

TAUKKYAN

17th Ind. Division
Rangoon Garrison
withdrawal 7th Mar.

INSEIN

N

Japanese enter
RANGOON
morning 8th Mar.

On the 6th March, the day after his arrival, General
Alexander realised that if the Rangoon Garrison and 17th
Indian Division were to be saved, an immediate withdrawal
was essential. Owing to the Japanese infiltration north of
Pegu, there was only one way out and that was by the Prome
road. This only involved a direct movement north for the
Rangoon Garrison but for 17th Indian Division this was far
more difficult and dangerous (See Diagram.) They had to
retreat south westwards down the main Pegu-Rangoon road,

then by a minor road across the Rangoon-Prome road at Taukkyan; this area was the scene of the miracle of 'the Armies that passed in the night' which will be enlarged upon at the end of this chapter.

The day of our departure dawned at last. We received our orders for evacuation on the morning of the 7th March and by midday it became obvious that something had gone wrong with the land evacuation to Prome. The rumour was that the Army Headquarters' courier on his way to Maymyo, very early in the morning, had got through but the first part of the Rangoon Garrison had been stopped just north of Taukkyan by a Japanese road block. This was of no great concern to us personally, as we had been told that the final demolitions were timed for the early afternoon and the 'last ditchers' would be taken off the riverside wharfs and ferried to the waiting ships at about 4 p.m. However, fate decreed otherwise.

The Military Governor arrived at about 2 p.m. at the Mogul Guard, with fresh orders. According to him, the ships were overcrowded and we were, therefore, to proceed north by road. He concluded by informing us that a company of the Gloucesters would be coming over from Syriam (the oil refinery) across the Rangoon River that evening and that they and the remainder of the Rangoon Garrison would go out together. We could go with them; we should be all right. My immediate reaction was one of anger at this breach of faith towards my men but there was nothing which I could do to remedy matters. It was just lucky that we had not yet burnt our vehicles and could, therefore, be independent – at least as far as transport was concerned.

I was sitting with Prescott at about 3 p.m. when the fan suddenly stopped and this was immediately followed by the boom of an explosion – the power station had been blown up to render it useless to the enemy. The sound of further explosions came from various parts of the city and from along the waterfront. The Police party moved down to the wharf shortly after and we were left pretty well alone in

Rangoon, as the only others going by land were the railway party. They were planning to take a train north on the Prome line in the early evening.

There was now no point in remaining any longer at the Mogul Guard so we packed up and moved our small party to the riverside area. Here, to our astonishment, we found a British Lieutenant of the Royal Indian Navy; the peak of his cap had been nearly blown off and he was in possession of a jeep painted battleship grey and labelled HMIS *Hindustan*. He explained that he had been doing demolition work and had missed the last launch and we accordingly invited him to join our party. He accepted with alacrity and rewarded us with the information that there was beer in the refrigerator of the Port Trust Club and, as the electricity had not long been off, it should still be cold.

We parked our vehicles in front of the now deserted fire station, collected chairs from inside and proceeded to sit on the pavement and drink our beer, more as though we were in some Continental cafe instead of being in the eerie position of the last inhabitants of a deserted and partially destroyed city.

The launches with the Gloucesters came in at last and after a good deal of sorting out, they embussed and joined the remainder of the Rangoon Garrison. I reported to the Major commanding the column and was told to fall in my party behind the second company and before the rear guard. We moved through the city and across the bridge at the west end of the railway station on to the Prome road. I took the time and remember that it was shortly after 7.30 p.m.

There has been some controversy over who were the last out of Rangoon and I have always maintained that it was our party. The Official History, however, says that the last train left at 7.30 p.m. but I think that we were slightly behind them. The real truth concerning an event can seldom be assessed so let it suffice to say that this honour belongs to either the railway party or ourselves or it could belong to both.

A number of totally incorrect reports circulated soon after the evacuation, one being that a huge mob of evacuees had collected at the riverside and that as the last boats pulled away, the waiting Burmese fell upon them and massacred the lot. This was absolute nonsense; complete order was maintained until several hours after the last launches had left and no known evacuees were abandoned. The Official History makes no mention of our road party whatsoever and by giving the train departure time as 7.30 p.m., by inference makes this the last party out. However, when dealing with the Navy's role in the evacuation, the Official History talks of the departure of the ship *Heinrich Jensens* on the morning of the 8th March, after embarking the demolition parties. Whether this vessel moved down the Rangoon River during darkness on the 7th evening or at first light on the 8th March I do not know but I do know that all demolition parties had left Rangoon by about 5 p.m. on the 7th March.

It was quite dark by the time we had cleared Rangoon City and on reaching a point about three miles out where the road forked, the leading three or four lorries took the left fork, the Insein road, by mistake and the column ground to a halt. My little party consisting of my staff car (a requisitioned Ford V8), a Field Security jeep, the Royal Indian Navy jeep and a Field Security 15 cwt truck was well down the column and we were ignorant of what had happened ahead. After a while I took the jeep up to the front and found the Column Commander and his officers in a huddle, trying to find a way of backing the whole column so as to allow the erring vehicles to get back on to their correct road.

The darkness added to the confusion so I suggested that as the left fork went to Prome, via Insein, instead of via Taukkyan, we should continue. This made no difference to me as I was only interested in getting to Prome and then on to Maymyo. The Column Commander objected; he had been ordered to rejoin his unit at Taukkyan and to Taukkyan he was going. I could not argue against this, so, with a great deal of trouble and cursing, we eventually got the column sorted out and on the right road. What I did not know was how kind Fate, in the person of the Column Commander, had been that night. If we had continued up the road to Insein, we should have run headlong into the Japanese.

We arrived at Taukkyan somewhere about 9 p.m. I found Army Headquarters and reported to Philip Gwyn. The atmosphere was somewhat on the gloomy side. The whole of 17th Indian Division and the Rangoon Garrison, together with the Tactical part of Army Headquarters were now in an area of about one square mile, apparently hemmed in by the Japanese. The most unruffled man in the whole set up appeared to be the Army Commander himself. He was sitting quite imperturbably in a Burmese house, with nothing to lighten the darkness except a few oil lamps, apparently completely unconcerned that his command of the Army in Burma appeared unlikely to last for more than a few days.

Philip Gwyn took me aside and gave me a resumé of the situation. We had battered at the road-block all day without success. He added more comfortingly that the attacks had been very piecemeal, that is a company, then a company again, a battalion and then a battalion again, but on the following morning, at first light, 17th Indian Division with the tanks would mount a divisional attack and he concluded: 'Either we burst out like a cork out of a bottle or we go into the bag. In that event, I am putting on my boots and walking; I won't let the Japs capture me.' At this time I was almost ignorant of Japanese methods and told him I thought this a bit drastic and he said, 'They know about me from Shanghai and I really should be for it!'

After this, having nothing else to do, I got some food and then went to sleep near my car. I remember that I slept reasonably well until I was awakened by the noise of the tanks and of the Divisional attack forming up. I got up, had some tea and something to eat and as there was nothing for me to do for two or three hours, I made myself comfortable on the side of the road and read. I have often been asked why I did this and what was the name of the book that could so absorb me but odd as it may seem, I cannot answer either question for I do not know, all I do know is that the book passed the time while the attack was going on.

There were the usual noises of battle but, on the whole, not as strident as I should have expected and after a while transport began to move forward. I was under no one's direct command, in fact, I was merely 'on passage' to rejoin the rest of my staff at Maymyo, so I formed up my Field Security column and we moved forward in the general stream of traffic. After a while we passed the site of the road-block which, by now, had been demolished although there were few other signs of battle. Gradually we left behind the fighting units who were re-grouping and forged ahead northwards. We passed Prome and Magwe on that day and, in the late afternoon, stopped at a Government Rest House just north of the latter place. The beauty and peace of the countryside round about was in sharp contrast to our life and surroundings of the last few weeks and I wished that I could have stayed there for a few days in happier circumstances.

The next morning we were off again, through Yenangyaung and Mandalay, and climbing into the Shan Hills until, in the early evening, we reached Maymyo. The first period of the retreat was over for me, but to complete the picture I must revert to the extraordinary events of the night of the 7th March at the Taukkyan Bend and explain what had actually happened.

On first hitting the road-block above Taukkyan, our troops naturally concluded that the Japanese had done a flank march and had set up the block with the intention of preventing our withdrawal north. The fact that it was stubbornly defended all through the day, lent colour to this theory, but when the big attack went in on the morning of the 8th March, the road block was deserted and not a single Jap was to be seen.

It is now known that the Japanese thought that 17th Indian Division was withdrawing down the Pegu-Rangoon road to reinforce Rangoon, which they still assumed the

British were going to hold. To gain a quick victory, they decided not to pursue our Division but to do a right hook across the Prome road and down the Insein road, to arrive at Rangoon while our troops were still coming in and before they could take up their defensive positions. The road-block was simply a flank protection to the right hook. The result was that while we were concentrated at Taukkyan, a considerable Japanese force was passing within five miles of us. At the time we were attacking an empty road-block, the Japanese were mounting an attack on an equally empty Rangoon. Mercifully my suggestion that we should take the Insein Road was ignored.

V

Interlude in Maymyo

Maymyo – we arrived in the early evening, tired and dusty, and without any idea of how or where we should be accommodated. Imagine our joy, therefore, when on entering the town area we were greeted by a shout of welcome from Templar Widdicombe and Logan Gates, who had guessed that we should be arriving at about this time and had come out on the off chance of meeting us. Templar had already made all the necessary arrangements for our accommodation. MacGilp and his section were to go to the Bush Warfare School and I was to be accommodated with the Intelligence Staff in a small Mess which had been set up in a house in the Burma Rifles area of the Cantonment. Templar had used his knowledge and influence, as an old officer of Burma Army Headquarters, to take over a large, senior officer's married quarter. This was a double-storeyed house, fully furnished, giving us comfortable sitting- and dining-rooms and by doubling up and using the dressing-rooms as bedrooms, could accommodate us all. We each had a civilian servant and Templar had engaged a cook and laid in a good stock of food and drink. We were very much more comfortable than those accommodated in the makeshift Headquarter Officers' Messes. Philip Gwyn had to go into the Senior Officers' Mess, in order to be within easy reach should the General want him. The only disadvantage of our Mess was that it was at the opposite end of the town to Army

Headquarters; this caused some difficulties later on when petrol began to run short.

This period might be called an interlude between two retreats – that from Rangoon and that to India – a time of comparative calm for us, lasting until about 20th April, although this is not to say that we were idle. We used the lull to raise and train three further Field Security Sections and to get them into positions where they could be of most use.

In contrast to our comfortable, if busy existence, the fighting troops were continuously engaged in trying to stem the Japanese push northward. I have said that the 1st Burma Division, on being relieved by the Chinese VIth Army, moved from the Southern Shan States to the Sittang Valley to block any northward move of the Japanese from Pegu. This Division made some limited but successful southward attacks, which greatly assisted the withdrawal of 17th Indian Division. The arrival of the Chinese Vth Army in Burma led to a regrouping; 1st Burma Division was moved over to the Irrawaddy Valley and the Chinese took over the Sittang Valley front. At the same time a Corps Headquarters, with a commander, Lieutenant-General William Slim, was sent from India to take over as Bur-corps the 1st Burma Division and 17th Indian Division. By about 16th March, Bur-corps had 17th Indian Division in front of Prome and 1st Burma Division echeloned behind it, to protect the Yenangyaung oilfields. The Chinese Vth Army was to concentrate in the Toungoo area and the VIth Army was to do the same in the Southern Shan States.

The next disaster was in the air. The loss of Rangoon and its airfields gave the Japanese an advance base for their aircraft and left the British without any efficient warning system for their main base at Magwe. On the 20th March, after a successful raid by the RAF and AVG on Mingaladon airfield at Rangoon, the Japanese retaliated in force that same afternoon and on the following morning, by attacking Magwe and destroying a large number of British aircraft on the ground and causing havoc generally. They proceeded to do the same at Akyab on the following day. It was only prudent, therefore, to withdraw Headquarters 'Burwing' RAF and AVG to Lashio, and Headquarters 'Akwing' to Chittagong and the remaining RAF and AVG aircraft to India and China, respectively. It was the only action possible in the circumstances, but the complete absence of any air support in the following days, caused bitter resentment among the fighting troops and a situation resulted which was akin to that which existed between the Army and RAF at the time of Dunkirk. This situation was not improved by the alleged circumstances of the RAF withdrawal from Magwe. The Official History infers that it was an orderly and systematic move out but all the reports I received from both civil and military intelligence sources, spoke of a near panic and disgruntled reports were current of the lack of any effort to salvage equipment or to destroy documents. It must be said that detachments did return later to clear up the mess and to staff Magwe as a forward landing ground but by that time the damage had been done. The accuracy or inaccuracy of these stories will probably never be proved but, at the time, they were widely believed by the Army and did little to sustain morale.

Once the Japanese had command of the air, they ranged unopposed over the whole of Burma but their attacks were directed more at disorganising such normal life as was still continuing than attacking the fighting formations. They bombed the larger towns continually, although Maymyo escaped with only one light raid. In these raids, the towns were almost completely destroyed, either by the bombs or, as the buildings were almost entirely made of wood, by the resultant fires. In the absence of any allied air power, they were able also to strafe at will railway installations, trains and river steamers. All this helped to accelerate the cessation of normal life and, as at Rangoon, there were no troops available to maintain communications and essential services, these ground to a halt.

It is difficult to assess the effectiveness of this policy. There is no doubt that it added greatly to our difficulties behind the front line but, beyond being a great nuisance and a hindrance to the maintenance of our fighting forces, it is doubtful if it contributed actively to our defeat. On at least two occasions such as the Battle of Yenangyaung and at the final withdrawal across the Irrawaddy by ferry and the Ava Bridge, determined air attacks on our formations might well have turned the retreat into a disaster comparable to that at the Sittang River earlier in the campaign. On the fronts held by the Chinese things were different. The lack of transport and the Chinese reliance on civilian communications, particularly the railway, made their Armies more vulnerable to this form of attack.

The Japanese pushed relentlessly on during this period, defeating 17th Indian Division at Prome and 1st Burma Division at Yenangyaung. This latter action was nearly a disaster and the Burma Division was only saved by the high fighting qualities of the 38th Division of the recently arrived Chinese LXVIth Army and the competence of its Commander, General Sun Li Jen. On the other fronts the Japanese soon pushed the Chinese out of Toungoo, and this gave them command of a lateral road into the Southern Shan States. Relentlessly they continued to push the Vth Army northwards and moved considerable forces into the Shan States, where they inflicted several defeats on the VIth Army. Unfortunately, owing to the defects in the Chinese system of command, the state of affairs on the VIth Army front was not known to either the Chinese Headquarters or Headquarters Burma Army until too late.

The whole of this unhappy time was notable for its lost opportunities; on at least two occasions a chance occurred to deal strong counter-attacks on the flanks of the Japanese who had penetrated deeply on one or other of the fronts. In each case the lack of co-operation, dilatoriness and often complete disregard of orders by the Chinese Commanders, made these attacks abortive.

It is difficult to put any definite estimate on how much or

how little effect the Chinese Armies had on the campaign. There is no doubt that without them the attenuated British forces would have been quite unable to hold the three fronts of the Irrawaddy, Sittang and the Shan States, and the Japanese would have overrun the whole of Burma in a matter of weeks or even days, rather than months. On the other hand, had the Chinese Commanders co-operated to the full, both with the British forces and with each other, and had they obeyed the orders, given by their own High Command, with reasonable promptitude, the Japanese could well have been dealt severe blows. These might well have so slowed up their advance that, by the time the monsoon broke in May and which temporarily would have brought campaigning to a halt, large portions of Burma might have remained in British and Chinese hands. It is not intended to probe further but much of the trouble originated from the Generalissimo himself, who daily changed the command structure, and the trepidation of most of the Chinese Generals which led them to refer back to the Generalissimo for confirmation, every order received. The indiscipline of most of the Chinese formations and their habit of shooting all Burmese on sight, led to innumerable difficulties, and this at a time when so much of their supplies and transportation depended on civil government agencies.

By about the 20th April, Bur-corps and the Chinese Vth Army were back on the general line Chauk–Kyaukpadaung–Meiktila–Thazi and there, for the moment, the Japanese advance appeared to have been slowed up. On the VIth Army front the position was obscure but there was no reason to believe that any major disaster had occurred.

However, to return to the activities of the Intelligence Staff and the Field Security Sections during this period of about six weeks. The Intelligence Staff, as mentioned earlier, was most comfortably housed in one of the loveliest places in Burma – the glorious scenery and the temperate climate I shall always remember with pleasure. The town itself was largely untouched by war and owing to its open development, escaped the attention of the Japanese who preferred to bomb the crowded wooden tenements of the larger cities. The Club was still open with its reasonably well-stocked bar, library and weekly dances, and it was within walking distance of our house. The forethought of General Hutton in back loading stores from Rangoon to the Mandalay–Shwebo area and the production of petrol at the small local refinery at Yenangyaung until the last possible moment, meant that for the time being at least, there was no great shortage of rations or petrol. This was reflected in our living standards. In the beginning we left our offices at Army Headquarters and returned to our bungalow for an excellent lunch prepared by our cook but later on we received peremptory orders from Philip Gwyn that in order to save petrol, this practice must stop. We were reluctant to take sandwiches to the office and instead decided to arrange to have a cold lunch brought to us by one of our servants; he hired one of the horse-drawn victorias which plied for hire in Maymyo. In addition to our rations we had locally produced vegetables, fowls and eggs were plentiful and the Mandalay Brewery was still producing an excellent light beer.

In the midst of this comparative peace and plenty, work was still essential and the immediate priority was to train as many Field Security Sections as was possible, bearing in mind the difficulty of finding suitable personnel and officers. An intensive ten-day crash course was started, and, while all of us shared in the instruction, the main brunt was borne by Tony Summersell, of whose drive and initiative I cannot speak too highly. During the whole of my time in Security Intelligence I knew a few Field Security Officers as good as Tony but none better.

The training and accommodation of these sections, while in Maymyo, brought us into collision with the Commandant of the Bush Warfare School, Major Calvert, later to become famous as a column commander of the Chindits – 'Mad Mike' Calvert. The Bush Warfare School was the cover name for an organisation training British Other Ranks as guerrillas for use in China, and friction arose as we were, to a certain extent, competing for the same small stock of personnel. 'Mad Mike' and his officers viewed our efforts with an amused contempt, which brought them into conflict with my Field Security Officers. However, these difficulties were smoothed over and finally ceased when the Field Security were moved out as Sections, to their various locations. I had judged, from the very beginning of the campaign, that the security of the rear areas was the first priority and now I had to decide where the Sections should be located to give the best service. These decisions had not only to be based on the present positions of our supply dumps and base organisations but be flexible enough also to allow for future changes and movements.

Early in April, Wavell had impressed on Alexander that, in the event of the loss of Burma, he should endeavour to hold as many 'entry points' into the country from India and China as possible, and to prevent any charge of the British having abandoned the Chinese, contact must be kept with them even if this meant splitting up the British forces. In conformity with this Directive, Alexander made a plan which involved splitting the British forces into three – 1st Burma Division would withdraw up the Ye U-Kalewa track, to cover the re-entry point from Manipur; 17th Indian Division, less one Brigade, would go north up the railway to Myitkyina, to cover the projected route from Upper Assam through the Hukaung Valley, later to become the Ledo Road, and the Armoured Brigade and one Brigade of 17th Indian Division would accompany the Chinese Vth Army up the Burma Road to Lashio. The VIth Army would retire on China with Lashio and Kengtung. The later military situation, however, made this plan abortive but it was the one we had to work on.

The first priority was Mandalay which together with Shwebo was our main supply and depot area. I intended to keep MacGilp's Section with me for the security of Army Headquarters and any special jobs which might occur. This was now re-named No. 1 Burma Composite Field Security Section. The next Section out, No. 2, I gave to Summersell and sent him off to Mandalay with orders that his withdrawal route would be with 1st Burma Division towards Kalewa. No. 3 Section was Acomb's and was sent to Lashio and No. 4, Mansfield's Section, went to the Katha–Myitkyina area. I gave the Field Security Officers a very careful briefing. I explained that, while it was hoped that we would hold the three re-entry points of Kalewa, Myitkyina and Lashio, there was always the possibility that the military situation might turn drastically against us. In this event, while Bill Talbot and I would do our best to keep in touch, each Field Security Officer would have to be responsible for the work and safety of his own Section. I impressed upon them that there was always the possibility of the retreat becoming a rout in one or other of the sectors and that at this juncture panic would ensue. In the event, each Field Security Officer must use his own judgement as to when and by what route he got his Section out. There would be innumerable ways in which he could assist the local Commanders and he must continue to do this for as long as possible. They carried out their orders both gallantly and well as all who had dealings with them can vouch.

It was obvious that I, myself, should have to visit the various areas in which my Field Security Sections would be working. The first area and the most accessible was Mandalay, only 40 odd miles away by a good, if winding road. I accompanied Philip Gwyn, who was going to give the staff of the local Line of Communication Sub Area some hints on how to deal with the Chinese, whose main supply base they were about to become. I fear that he upset the local Staff when he told them that the Chinese were quite unpredictable and that they should not be surprised if the Chinese Intelligence Officer dealt with the rice and the Supply Officer with Intelligence. They did not believe him, not unnaturally, but later events proved him not far wrong.

Mandalay was the second city of Burma and had been the

capital of the independent state of Upper Burma, which the British annexed after the Third Burma War. It was dominated by an enormous walled complex, which had formerly contained the palace of the last Kings, and was now named Fort Dufferin. This was a vast area which contained a hotchpotch of palaces, temples, barracks, military depots and the main military hospital. In peace time the entry of civilians to the palaces and temples may have caused a security headache, but in war the fact that it was surrounded by a wall and a moat and pierced by few gates made it a security asset. The concentration of so many military installations in a small area presented, however, an easy target for enemy bombers.

Immediately to the south of the Fort were the Civil Lines; this was the name given to the area which contained the administrative offices of the Mandalay Civil District, the Police barracks and the houses of the civil and railway officers, and of the European mercantile community. This area also contained the railway station with its engine shed and marshalling yards. Between the railway and the River Irrawaddy, with the wharves of the Irrawaddy Flotilla Company, was the native city – a tangle of narrow streets and wooden buildings. I felt sure that Summersell and his Section would have plenty to occupy them.

My next tour was to Lashio. This again was accomplished by road through the glorious scenery of the Shan States. The road ran roughly parallel with the railway and I was able to see the world famous viaduct over the Gokteik Gorge. This magnificent feat of engineering was unique in that two or three of the piers stood on a natural arch above the river at the bottom of the gorge and, therefore, it was possible to say that the viaduct was 350 feet from the bottom of the highest pier but 820 feet from the bed of the river. In Lashio I found little that was satisfactory and much that was bad. The town had the appearance of a boom town of the Mid West as portrayed in a western film. There was a small British garrison of the Burma Frontier Force, who were vainly trying to induce some order into the general chaos. Lashio being the railhead for the Burma–China road and the last town of any size before the Chinese border, enormous numbers of Burmans, Shans and Chinese had poured into the town to set up shops, hotels and eating houses in a frenzied get rich quick operation. Add to this various Chinese Army organisations and the tough guys of the AVG and the picture was complete. The local State authorities and the Police had long since given up any attempt to enforce normal standards of administration and conduct. Corruption, smuggling and graft were rife and I was certain that no military secret would remain so for more than a minute in this state of affairs. I had interviews with the staff of Station Headquarters and with the Police and promised to send up a Field Security Section as soon as possible. The night was spent in the Transit Mess, a most uncomfortable place and after Maymyo a bed in a dormitory had little to recommend it, however, the next morning I was able to return to Maymyo.

My next tour would have to be to the Shwebo and Ye U areas and this time I intended to travel in comfort, so I asked Colonel Brewitt, who had set up his Railway Headquarters in Mandalay, if he would let me have a Railway Officer's Saloon. This type of vehicle is largely non-existent in England, where Railway Officers can usually return to their homes each night, or, if they do have to stay away for a night can easily find accommodation. In the East, the great distances and paucity of hotels or other similar accommodation has caused the railway administration to provide a large stock of saloons. These varied from the palatial vehicles of the senior officers, to the four-wheelers of the junior staff. These latter were extremely comfortable; at one end of the coach was the main compartment, containing two sofa berths, a table, chairs and cupboards, rather like the interior of a modern caravan. A corridor led out of this, past the bathroom with its basin, shower and lavatory, to the servants' compartment; this was usually sub-divided into a kitchen with a sink and coal stove and the living space proper.

The saloon could be detached from the train at any station which had a siding and then re-attached to another train as required.

The railway administration allotted me a small bogie saloon with the same interior arrangements as a four-wheeler. I had intended to have it sent up to Maymyo but I subsequently got a message to say that for operating reasons, the railway administration would prefer me to join the saloon at Mandalay. I instructed Manuel, my servant, to pack up my gear, food and drink and we drove down to Mandalay, where I found that the saloon was already attached to the rear of the daily train to Myitkyina, and before long we were off southwards.

Mandalay is shown on maps as the junction of the Myitkyina and Lashio branches with the main line but the actual divergence takes place at one station south – Myohaung – some six miles from Mandalay proper. This station has only two running loops, therefore all trains from Rangoon or the branches continued on to Mandalay where they could be re-marshalled in the Mandalay Yard. We took the right hand road at the junction and soon were rumbling over the great Ava Bridge and shortly afterwards reached Ywataung, which was the junction for the Ye U branch. Ywataung was the Headquarters of a District of the Burma Railway administration and contained the offices of the District Traffic Superintendent, District Engineer and District Mechanical Engineer, with their houses and quarters for the staff. We had left Mandalay in the mid-morning and arrived at Shwebo in the early afternoon. Here my saloon was cut off from the train and parked in a siding and I then went off to Military Headquarters in a car which had been sent to meet me.

Shwebo was an ordinary 'District' town; that is a town which was the Headquarters of a Civil District, comprising the usual city and civil lines, but with the difference that in peace time it had a small military garrison, including a detachment of British troops. They were accommodated in a small cantonment about two miles from the town proper. After war broke out, this had been largely taken over by the 2nd Echelon of Burma Army – the section which deals with the documentation and records of soldiers on active service. These offices were staffed by a few officers and a vast number of Indian and Burmese clerks who, in the majority of cases, had their families with them. It was evident that the evacuation of this multitude would be a great problem if and when the time came. There was also an airfield which was in constant use by aircraft bringing reinforcements from India and taking out wounded and such European women and children as had still not left the country. The incoming and outgoing were accommodated in transit camps in the cantonment area.

Life in Shwebo, other than the changes mentioned above, was practically normal and there were none of the problems which bedevilled Lashio and Mandalay. In the evening I returned to the saloon and arranged with the Station Master to have it attached to the train for Mandalay which was coming through during the night. It was my intention to proceed on the following day to Ye U but for some reason, now forgotten, I decided to carry on through to Mandalay rather than have the saloon detached at Ywataung and to await the Ye U train there. This decision was to have surprising repercussions.

I awoke to find my saloon in Mandalay station and, after breakfast, I arranged for it to be shunted on to the Ye U train which was due to depart at about 11 a.m. The saloon was attached in front, immediately behind the engine, and the train was drawn up on the principal platform. The platforms at Mandalay station ran north and south, with the principal road, No. 1, adjacent to the main station buildings. There were some four platform roads and parallel to the platform roads was the marshalling yard. This was full to overflowing with wagons laden with every type of store evacuated from the south. The railway administration were still trying, although with a very depleted staff, to sort them out and work them away to the various depots where they were needed and could be unloaded. Unfortunately owing to the haste with which they were loaded, few wagons were properly labelled and so the contents and destinations were largely unknown.

The starting signal was off at about 11 o'clock and I was sitting in the saloon squeezing lemons, intending to add the juice to some gin for a pre-lunch drink, when there was the most tremendous explosion. My first impression was that the engine had blown up but then there came a second explosion, closely followed by a third and by then I realised that an air raid was in progress – my instinctive reaction was to dive under the berth. On reflection some time later, I realised that the woodwork of the body of the saloon could hardly have kept out bomb splinters and that the floor height of a metre gauge coach was just right to receive the maximum amount of blast from a bomb bursting near by. The explosions soon ceased and I emerged on to the platform. It was quite impossible to see anything as the dust raised by the bombing was worse than a desert sandstorm. The dust was only just beginning to settle when down came another stick of bombs. This time I raced down the platform to the Station Master's office which had a baffle wall in front of its doors. In my haste I slipped on the broken glass which littered the platform from the shattered roof and came down, cutting a nasty gash in my hand. The Japanese raids at this time were comparatively short and concentrated, as the bombers came over in waves and each wave released its bombs simultaneously; this type of bombing they considered to be the most effective in terrorising the civil population. As soon as the dust had settled again and those of us who were on the station had recovered our wits, we took stock of the situation.

The damage, fortunately, was comparatively light as the Japanese were using high fragmentation anti-personnel bombs and the first bombs had landed ahead of the engine of my train for the sticks had fallen diagonally from south-east to north-west across the yard. By the time the bombs were falling on a level with my saloon, several lines of steel goods trucks were between me and the explosion, and this undoubtedly saved my life. The craters were small and the damage done to the track was minimal and could be put right in a short time. Mercifully the bombs had not fallen on the actual station or its approaches, or the loss of life would have been very heavy. There had been no warning whatsoever and the platform and forecourt were crammed with passengers, food vendors and beggars – all the usual turbid conglomeration of a normal Eastern station. The main danger seemed to be from one or two small fires in the marshalling yard.

There was a shunting engine in steam, with a driver, at the north end of the yard but the signalman not unnaturally though very unfortunately, had decamped. The north signal box, although small, was fully interlocked and the points and signals remained locked unless they were pulled in the correct sequence. Colonel Brewitt and other railway officers arrived on the scene but no one had any knowledge of the interlocking sequence – so – the projected use of the shunting engine to pull the wagons away from the fire had to be abandoned in favour of manpower – we pushed the wagons. After a fairly lengthy session of wagon pushing, my hand became extremely painful and was bleeding quite freely; Brewitt suggested that it was time to let the Railway Doctor have a look at it. The railway authorities had a dispensary in a bungalow immediately in front of the main station forecourt and I went to it. The doctor put in the necessary stitches, bandaged up my hand and told me to go over to the adjacent Railway Officers' Mess where they would give me something to drink. I was just approaching the Mess when I happened to notice a slit trench and simultaneously there was another tremendous explosion. Now whether I jumped into the slit trench or was blown into it by the blast, I shall never know, but as I went in I became aware that the whole front of the Mess was bulging out and collapsing. After a while, when all seemed quiet again, I got out of the trench and saw that the station had become a total wreck; the buildings were a shambles, the overbridge had come down and badly damaged coaches and trucks were lying about in heaps like so many broken toys. It later transpired that the damage had been done by a wagon load of RAF bombs which no one had known were there, exploding in the fire.

This incident effectively put paid to any idea of going to Ye U by train, in fact, Mandalay station was never used again during the campaign; all trains terminated at Myo-haung station to the south and the administration moved over to the District Offices at Ywataung. I went off to see Summersell in order to get some assessment of the situation in Mandalay City. This was grim indeed; the town had liter-ally ceased to exist. The small Japanese bombs which caused so little damage to the station, had wreaked the most fearful havoc in the overcrowded, narrow streets of wooden houses in the city. Fires had started and with no means of contain-ing them, the whole city area was literally burnt out. The total number of casualties could never be ascertained, it probably ran into thousands. The warning system had com-pletely broken down and the sirens had not been sounded. Until this raid Mandalay had been largely untouched by the war and the bazaars were crowded with local inhabitants and villagers from the surrounding countryside: now it was a ruin with hoards of terrified people streaming out of it in every direction.

The best account of this tragedy, that I know of, was actually written at the time and is contained in a telegram sent by Alfred Wagg, an American War Correspondent, on the evening of that day:

'Friday April third Mandalay Dash Japanese bombers thirty-six bombed for three hours beginning eleven a.m. this morning ancient and holy city of Mandalay now the first Burmese city is in flames Stop Japs poured down incendiaries and anti-personnel and high explosives which began conflagration which destroyed commercial centre and laid waste two-thirds of city proper Stop First report unofficial and incomplete on account of continuing fires place dead from two to three thousand and wounded approximately five thousand Stop Aircraft approached city from north-easterly direction at around five to six thousand feet Stop Civilians not warned of air raid were conducting business as usual when bombs burst accounting for large numbers of dead and injured Stop Streets filled with those trapped who were incinerated alive Stop Station was hit by incendiaries setting off trainload of RAF bombs standing in railway yard which smashed and wrecked Stop Hit ammunition dumps and oilcars on sidings put water and electric systems out of commission rendering operations by doctors impossible and also hit civil hospital Stop Over Lower Burma Road towards Lashio thousands are seeking safety in country where now masses of civilians are homeless Stop Insufficient ARP no appreciable fire department except few hoses near fort along historic moat reason why fire spread Stop Eye saw time bombs exploding hours after last plane departed Stop During entire raid no RAF in sight Stop Picture city which since my arrival in Burma held my interest and imagination now sixth in systematic series of Jap raids on communication supplies and civilians leaving towns and cities aflame – WAGG.'

As soon as things had quietened down a little, I arranged for my kit which fortunately for me was still in existence, to be moved from the station to the Field Security house. I was even luckier in finding my servant, Manuel, alive and well. He had vanished when the bombing started and now his only comment on the whole proceedings was – 'Too much bombing Sah – too much bombing!'

During the afternoon I toured the Mandalay area with Summersell and saw nothing but disaster and devastation. Since nothing was to be gained by staying on, later in the evening Manuel and I set out for Maymyo in a Field Security jeep. I sat in front with the driver and Manuel was in the back with my kit. On arrival at Maymyo, I noticed that Manuel was a bit slow in getting out of the jeep and decidedly unsteady on his feet. I questioned him about his condition and the only reaction from Manuel was a broad grin and a somewhat indistinct reiteration of his previous statement, 'Too much bombing Sah – hic – toooo mush bombing!' It transpired that in the forty-two miles from Mandalay he had drunk the best part of a bottle of my gin. There was nothing to be done just then so I let him shamble off to his quarters and thought that we had seen the last of him for that night. An incorrect assumption on my part for, halfway through dinner, the other servants complained that he was creating a nuisance in the pantry. I went out to deal with him and was greeted with the familiar refrain: 'TOO MUCH BOMBING!' so taking him by the scruff of his neck, I started to march him to the tap. Unfortunately, he tripped over the step and fell down with me on top of him – no light weight. He then passed out cold. Next morning he arrived with my tea, apparently none the worse for his over enthusiastic potations and other adventures.

The days continued quietly enough in Maymyo for although Bur-corps and the Chinese Vth Army were gradually forced back towards Mandalay, there was always hope that by the time the monsoon broke, General Alexander's plan of holding the three re-entry points would have taken effect.

It was during this period that I made contact with Chinese Army Headquarters and received from them a most elaborate 'pass'. Until now it had not been translated so I was in ignorance of its meaning, but it did smooth my path which was really all that I required of it.

On another occasion the Generalissimo Chiang Kai-shek, himself, visited Maymyo and the Burma Railways managed to provide him with a luxurious special train of saloon coaches to transport him to and from Lashio. It fell to my lot to lead a party to search this train for any explosive devices or other possible forms of sabotage and I deputed a Field Security escort to travel with it, not entirely in order to safeguard the Great Man but more in order to safeguard the railway men from the ill behaviour of the Chinese of the Generalissimo's escort.

It is possible that perhaps I spent more time than I should at the railway station on this and other duties but the operation of this difficult section of line always had something of interest to me as a student of railways. Trains from Mandalay came up the hill section with an articulated Garrett locomotive at their head; on the way up the locomotive pushed its train from one reversing station to the next and in this way any turning round of locomotives at the two reversing stations was obviated. On arrival at Maymyo the Garretts were taken off and another large locomotive of the Mallet type was substituted to take the train on to Lashio.

I made one last trip to Mandalay and this for a very special purpose. News had got round that the management of the Mandalay Brewery were about to evacuate so, if we wanted any more beer now was the time to get it. Everyone I knew gave me money to make purchases on their behalf and on arrival at the brewery I loaded up the jeep with as many cases as it could possibly hold. The actual number of cases escapes my memory but I do recollect that they bulged over the jeep's sides and had to be secured by ropes and chains. A jeep is a short based vehicle and to drive one up a winding mountain road with such a weight on the rear rendered it almost unmanageable – mine swayed all over the road just as if it too were 'on the beer'.

The Burma Police had provided me with an interpreter and liaison officer while I was in Maymyo. His name was Rivers and he was a Sergeant of the Mandalay District Police. He was an Anglo-Burmese and was my constant companion, acting as 'guide, philosopher and friend' until we finally reached India.

In Maymyo we had been very much more fortunate than many others but on about 25th April news was received which put an end to our comparative ease, we were to be on the move again.

VI

Collapse

Philip Gwyn returned from the usual morning operations conference and immediately I saw from his face that something had gone wrong – and it had. The Chinese VIth Army had been routed in the Southern Shan States; for about a week they had endured daily Japanese attacks, which they had neither repulsed nor held their ground. Nevertheless in spite of these daily withdrawals their Headquarters had continued to send out optimistic and reassuring communiques, with the result that when they finally broke their line was considerably behind where Army Headquarters had expected them to be. We, therefore, might expect to find the Japanese astride the Lashio road and railway around Gokteik in a day or so.

Any attempt to hold the re-entry points was now out of the question; all that could be done was to save as many troops as possible, for the later defence of India. The original plan was scrapped and Bur-corps told to disengage from the enemy and retreat behind the Irrawaddy for a final retirement up the Ye U–Kalewa track. It was hoped that the 38th Division of the Chinese LXVIth Army would accompany the British forces to India on this axis, while the Chinese Vth Army were to be sent up the Lashio road to block the Japanese advance and keep the road open for the time being. All these moves caused considerable confusion on the road and railway, particularly between Maymyo and Mandalay, where the British and Chinese forces were moving in opposite directions on a single line railway and a mountain road.

Philip Gwyn told me that Army Headquarters would be moving to Shwebo that day but I was to remain for a day or two with MacGilp's Section to do various odd jobs. One of these jobs was to supervise the security aspect of the move of Army Headquarters, notably that no documents of value to the enemy were left behind. There had already been a case where documents left behind by a senior officer of Burcorps Headquarters had been recovered by the Field Security and we did not want a recurrence.

The law and order aspect in Maymyo also required watching in case of a breakdown while the evacuation was taking place, and the influx of large bodies of Chinese troops on their way to Lashio was of little assistance in this respect. There was one task, however, which I had to undertake on that day, the results of which had no small repercussion. A large petrol dump was situated a few miles from Mandalay on the Maymyo railway line and it contained high octane fuel for the Armoured Brigade; my GSO I gave me direct and peremptory orders, which he had received, personally from General Alexander, to go and destroy the petrol at once – which I did. It was the first time I had had the experience of burning a petrol dump and a terrifying one it proved to be – exploding drums of petrol flew about and scattered flames in every direction. These orders had been given on the strict understanding that the Armoured Brigade had already collected what petrol they needed and could carry back but regrettably this assumption was incorrect. The Armoured Brigade transport arrived that same evening only to find a scene of complete devastation. This led to bitter recriminations against Army Headquarters, not unnaturally, but of all this I was mercifully completely ignorant until years later when I read Field Marshal Lord Slim's book, 'Defeat into Victory', in which he makes some extremely scathing remarks about a 'staff officer from Army Headquarters'. I happened to mention this to him at a Gurkha Brigade Dinner but in spite of my explanations that I had only acted under direct orders from General Alexander, he was still 'not amused'.

We returned to Maymyo that evening, visiting the reversing stations on the railway on our way back. We found these deserted and looted and with the block signalling instruments smashed. The track was intact but the lack of staff and signalling made two-way movement on the railway both difficult and hazardous. Maymyo was almost deserted but some reassurance came from hearing the buglers of the Depot of the Burma Rifles blowing the 'Last Post' and then 'Lights Out', although, in the circumstances, these calls might have been thought to be prophetic.

The next day I had to deal with the problem of two civil security prisoners. One of these was a Dane, a Mr Ebbe Munch, and the other an NCO of the Vichy French Forces. Munch had crossed the Indo-China–Burma border as a private individual and, failing to convince the Chinese Army authorities in the Shan States of his *bona fides*, was arrested and handed over to the civil authorities in Maymyo. He was a nephew of a former Prime Minister of Denmark and although probably perfectly innocent, his very presence in war time, as he moved about in the back of beyond of the Far East apparently aimlessly, was in itself suspicious. He had had in his possession a very large sum of money, in cheques, currency and gold. It was the loss of the latter somewhere 'along the line' that caused long and involved correspondence between the Danish Consulate, Headquarters Burma Army (in exile) and myself which lasted well into 1943.

The Vichy NCO had also been arrested by the Chinese after he had crossed the Burma border in Kentung, either by accident or design. He was sent up to Maymyo and both men were held on civil charges of illegal entry. This was a holding charge while they were being interrogated by the Burma Defence Bureau, an organisation similar to MI5 in England or the Intelligence Bureau of the Government of India, presided over by a Deputy Inspector General of the Burma Police, Lieutenant-Colonel C. G. Stewart. He, unfortunately, had no jail or warders to safeguard his prisoners owing to the general collapse of civil government, and so these two men were lodged in the Guard Room of the British Infantry Depot. However, they could not stay there for long as the Depot was moving out and as someone had to arrange for their removal to Shwebo, once again it was the Field Security who had to provide men to act as escort and the necessary transport.

In fact the Depot was not so much moving out as dissolving itself; all completely fit men were being sent to their units and the hospital was discharging any man who was fit enough to walk and carry a rifle. These men were being hastily organised into a British Composite Battalion, under Mike Calvert. They were intended to be used for guarding the Ye U–Kalewa track from Japanese infiltrators.

I completed what remained for me to do in Maymyo and then set off for Shwebo by easy stages. On the way I called in on Summersell and his Section; they were still in Mandalay. He was his usual cheerful self, although almost hidden by an enormous streamer covered with Chinese characters which was pinned to his shirt. He explained that this was a pass, without which he could not move about amongst the Chinese soldiers, who for reasons best known to themselves, were busily engaged in knocking holes in the walls of Fort Dufferin and my first thought was that there would be a row about this when the Government of Burma returned after the war. We agreed that Tony's Section should remain in Mandalay for as long as there were any British forces there and he was able to give assistance to the local authorities; after that he should go back as far as Kalewa and put himself at the disposal of the Line of Communication Headquarters. He would, therefore, leapfrog over No. 1 Section, which would go with me to Shwebo. I had been unable to make contact with Nos. 3 and 4 Sections but relied on Acomb and Mansfield to obey their orders and to do their best in whatever circumstances they might find themselves.

Continuing on towards Shwebo, that afternoon found me at the Railway Headquarters at Ywataung. Colonel Brewitt was still in control and asked me to stay the night; a suggestion which I accepted gladly because amongst other things I wanted to find out how best we could help him and his depleted staff for, by this time, they had come near to breaking point. He asked me, early in the evening, if I would take a party back over the Ava Bridge to help at Myohaung Junction Station south of Mandalay, where an air raid had caused difficulties and where the presence of a Chinese troop train was in no way improving the situation.

The bombing raid had taken place earlier in the day and although the tracks and main buildings of the station were intact, the signal box had received a near miss and this had jammed the rodding of the points, making it impossible to move the levers. The only way of moving the points was by unbolting the rods, moving them over by hand, and then re-bolting the rods. This was the job which the railway officers wanted the Field Security to carry out. The Chinese troop train was standing in one of the three roads waiting to proceed, in due course, to Lashio. The Chinese, themselves, were in a thoroughly truculent mood, refusing to allow the engine to be moved or to co-operate with the railway authorities in any way. The surrounding countryside was an inferno, every building within sight was ablaze and fusillades of shots rang out from time to time. This was the work of the Chinese soldiers who had left their train and were amusing themselves by shooting or burning any Burmese they could find. It never became clear to me why the Chinese took up this attitude towards the Burmese.

We had to push through a crowd of Chinese soldiers before we could get into the station office where we found two railway officers and from them we were able to elucidate the facts of the situation. It appeared that the Chinese troop train could not go up to Maymyo as a British ammunition train for Shwebo was coming down, and it was essential to get it through during the hours of darkness. Once the ammunition train was in, it, in its turn, could not proceed towards Shwebo as the daily train from Myitkyina was due. The block telegraph was not working so we had no exact knowledge of where these trains were or when they were likely to arrive. To make matters worse, one of the three running roads was too short to accommodate the expected trains and the Chinese were refusing to allow their engine to be uncoupled in order to proceed to the next station to get water. They were even threatening to shoot the driver should the engine be moved without their permission.

We engaged in a lengthy argument with the Chinese General but while we were arguing the Field Security men, under the direction of the railway officers, managed to alter the points so that the ammunition train could run into the other long road. Our attempts to explain matters to the Chinese were not so successful, in fact we had reached deadlock for their stock answer to everything was: 'Chinese Army fighting war, British Army not fighting war – Chinese go first!' Meanwhile the ammunition train arrived and it had not been in long before the Myitkyina train was heard whistling at the home signal on the other line. As if the existing situation was not bad enough, the crew of the ammunition train then told us that another supply train was following them down from Maymyo and that it would be unsafe to let the Chinese away until it had arrived.

We were now faced with a real railway puzzle, and one which would have been difficult enough to solve in normal circumstances. Two single lines, each with a train on it, facing a station of two lines each blocked by a train. Add to this darkness, bomb damage, lack of staff, no block telegraph and last but by no means least, your Allies threatening to shoot you and those working with you and you have a nightmare bad enough to daunt the bravest. However, a miracle, in the guise of a Senior British Officer of the Liaison Mission to the Chinese Armies, brought us relief. He accomplished this by the simple expedient of haranguing the Chinese

General with great fluency in his own language and in a very short time had reduced the General to order. Brewitt, meanwhile, had decided that the ammunition train must be got away at all costs; he instructed the train crew to back it up the Myitkyina line as far as the home signal, there to couple on to the incoming train, and thereafter the combined train was to back away over the Ava Bridge to Ywataung, and at Ywataung the two trains could be sorted out. Matters improved considerably from here on; the second train from Maymyo came in and this allowed the Chinese to be sent off towards Lashio, while we, in our turn, could return thankfully to Ywataung, there to sleep for what remained of the night.

The next day I motored on to Shwebo, where I found that on the Chinese fronts things were very bad indeed. The VIth Army had completely collapsed and, in spite of the superhuman efforts of General Stilwell to move units of the Vth Army to counter the Japanese advance on Gokteik, this had failed and the Japanese had cut the road, captured Lashio and were moving fast towards Bhamo. The effect of this was that most Chinese units on the Mandalay side of the Japanese, must now turn round and get over the Irrawaddy by the Ava Bridge, thus making this bottleneck even more congested. Luckily ferries were available, one to the north of Mandalay and one to the south of the Ava Bridge and these could take part of the Chinese forces and 1st Burma Division respectively.

The Staff at Shwebo were worried lest the breakdown of any vehicle on the actual bridge or its approach road, whether by mechanical defect or enemy air action, would inevitably cause such delays that the Japanese might arrive at the bridge before the withdrawal was complete and the Sittang disaster would then be repeated. In an effort to try to prevent this I was told to go back forthwith and do a reconnaissance of the bridge and its approaches, with a view to setting up an elaborate traffic control with marshalling areas, block posts, recovery units, etc., all linked to a control Headquarters by telephone. On completion I was to report back with my requirements of equipment and personnel.

By the time I had reached the bridge there was little daylight left and so it was the afternoon of the second day before I had completed my task and motored back to Shwebo, only to be told on arrival that my scheme was no longer required. Bur-corps had moved with great speed and skill and were practically all over the bridge and it seemed unlikely that there would be any interference from the enemy. The expected Japanese air attacks had not materialised and the few planes which did come over were met with such a barrage of light anti-aircraft fire that they prudently kept their distance.

This concentration of anti-aircraft guns at the bridge meant that there were none at Shwebo and as a result the few days we spent there were notable for the number of air raids we had to endure. Looking back, it seems that we spent most of our daylight hours in various ditches or culverts, as there were neither shelters nor slit trenches and no time to make them. During the course of these raids we got a direct hit on the I(b) office, destroying our last remaining files and records, and a near miss on the house in which we were billeted. In this latter incident one of our officers was killed and another survived only by a miracle. The survivor was a Lieutenant Ramamirthan, one of those unusual people who appear to have no sense of fear and in his case, I really believe this was true. 'Rama' was a South Indian Brahmin and he had been a Professor at Rangoon University but when this had closed he offered his services to the Army. He was a most remarkable man in that he had been a strict Hindu until he joined up, he had never eaten except under the ritual observances of his religion, which included amongst other things, no meat, the removal of his footwear and most of his clothing except for his dhoti or loincloth. His contacts with Europeans had been few and confined to his scholastic colleagues but now, almost without warning, he was pitchforked into a society of beef-eating, tough, not always immaculate British officers – a class which he had never before encountered but no one could have assimilated these changes with less fuss, or been more cheerful and helpful, or have shown greater courage than he did. Later on in the retreat General Alexander, himself, selected 'Rama' to work in the refugee staging camps on the Ye U–Kalewa track, where his unfailing cheerfulness and courage gave new heart to the refugees and undoubtedly saved many lives.

The Allied forces, meanwhile, were taking up their new positions; the Chinese forces were moving up the railway to the Katha area and Bur-corps were now in a general line along the banks of the Irrawaddy and Chindwin Rivers from Sagaing to Monwya. One brigade of 1st Burma Division was to the west of the Chindwin, preparing to withdraw up the Myittha Valley, to prevent the Japanese getting to Kalewa, by the back door, before we could reach it.

The Chinese forces, with the exception of Sun's 38th Division, were still a source of anxiety. They obstinately refused to obey any instructions given to them by the railway authorities and their habit of utterly disregarding warnings of trains coming in the opposite direction to theirs, finally brought all rail movement to a halt, as it was impossible to repair the damage caused by the inevitable accidents.

I heard later that up in the Katha area the Chinese arrested Colonel Brewitt and his railway officers, accusing them of sabotage when, owing to accidents and lack of staff, they were unable to comply with their requests. The situation became very ugly at one time and an operation was about to be mounted by the local British authorities to rescue them by force, using one of my Field Security Sections for the purpose, but luckily the Chinese had a change of heart and released Colonel Brewitt and his men.

Just before the end of the month orders came to get rid of all personnel not essential to the present operations and the final retreat to India. This involved an estimated number of about 2,400 persons – officers, civilians, clerks, servants, plus the families of many of them – now to be known as the 'useless mouths', who were to be taken by road to Ye U and

thence by rail south to the river port of Alon where river
steamers would convey them up the Chindwin to Kalewa.
As far as the Intelligence Branch was concerned, Widdicombe and Gates were to go with their staffs but the Army
Commander retained all the I(a) and I(b) officers, though
the few clerks still remaining to them were sent away. The
object of keeping relatively large numbers of officers of the
Intelligence Branch was that General Alexander intended to
use us as liaison officers to keep in touch with his formations,
should other communications break down.

The 'useless mouths' departed on the 29th April; we were
to start moving to a new Headquarters on the following day.
The first part of Burma Army Headquarters left Shwebo on
30th April, therefore, with the intention of setting up a new
Headquarters near Ye U. The departure of the 'useless
mouths' had cut our numbers drastically but even so there
was still too little transport to move the whole Headquarters
in one echelon and it was decided the move would have to
be made in two echelons on successive days. The transport
available was a motley collection of Army vehicles and
requisitioned civilians' cars of varied type and vintage. Con-
sequently, Army Headquarters did not, and in fact could
not, move as a tactical unit and the division into first and
second echelons was purely arbitrary.

I happened to be the commander of the first party which
consisted of about thirty persons – officers, soldier clerks,
civilian servants and about six or eight other ranks of the
Field Security. The latter, together with Sergeant Rivers, my
Police Liaison Officer, were what might be described as my
personal bodyguard. Rivers and I travelled in a Ford V8
saloon which was liberally plastered with mud as camouflage
against air reconnaissance.

My orders were to proceed to Ye U and then turn south
down the Monywa road for about five miles and set up Headquarters in a village. The selection of a village instead of the
relative comfort of a town, was a new departure and was an
attempt to get away from the daily bombing to which we

had been subjected at Shwebo.

We arrived at our village, without incident, in the early afternoon and found it deserted except for a few police. The village was the usual collection of wooden houses and huts, with a fort-like erection of brick and stone in the centre, which was the Police Station. At the time of our arrival, the local District Superintendent of Police was engaged in paying off the local force and telling them to go back to their homes until the British returned to Burma. This was soon accomplished and the Superintendent departed, leaving us in the deserted village. The only duty which had to be performed was to allot buildings to the various sections of Army Headquarters so that it could start functioning as soon as General Alexander arrived on the following day.

We put General Alexander and General Winterton (Major-General General Staff) in the Police Station and the Intelligence Staff was allocated a reasonable looking Burmese house close by. Apart from this we had nothing to do and the peace of that evening – no worries – no bombing, just tranquillity, is a memory I shall long treasure. I went to bed about 9 p.m. and was soon asleep. At about midnight I was awakened and told that something very curious was happening. There was a strong rumour that the Japanese had taken Monwya and although this seemed incredible, the rumour was seemingly confirmed by the fact that all the supply convoys which had left Ye U Supply Depot earlier had returned without delivering their loads.

I was completely at a loss to know what action I should or could take and my inclination was to attribute events to the Will of the Almighty and go to sleep again. However, since a group of officers surrounded me, all clamouring that I, as the senior, should at least issue *some* orders, there was nothing for it but to put on a brave face and act the part of a man with considerably more confidence than I actually possessed. I told them that the first thing to do was to try and find out whether we were in any immediate danger, and with this object in view we started down the road in two cars. The front car, which I drove myself, carried two of the best armed Field Security – one on each running board. The second car was driven by the GSO III Camouflage; in all we numbered about eight or ten men, armed with a far from conventional assortment of weapons – tommy guns, police shotguns and even police 'lathis'.

I confess that as we headed south with the possibility of running straight into the Japanese, my courage was at a very low ebb. My intention was to go about five miles down the road and then, if all was still clear of the enemy, to return to our village and go to bed. However, we had only gone about a mile along the road when we saw a vehicle coming towards us, its headlights blazing. We halted our two cars so that they blocked the road and hid behind trees, covering the road as completely as our limited fire power would allow. The vehicle stopped when it reached our cars and to our relief we saw that it was a 'Quad' of the Royal Indian Artillery, under the command of a Subaltern. We plied him with questions about the situation at Monwya and from his replies it appeared that the Japanese had appeared on the west bank of the Chindwin River, without the least warning, and had proceeded to mortar the town of Monwya. Although no great impact was made on the regular forces, a panic had broken out in the rear areas. This was alarming enough but the RIA Officer immediately reassured us by adding that the situation in and around Monwya had been restored, and as a further pacific he said that he had seen Bill Slim sitting down to dinner completely unruffled.

The panic which occurred at Alon on the Chindwin, about six miles above Monwya, was in large measure due to the fact that more than two thousand 'useless mouths' were concentrated there, awaiting transport northwards towards the Indian border. It spread to a detachment of the Burma Military Police and they, in turn, infected some of the drivers of the Subaltern's unit. He had been in pursuit of another vehicle which would be required to pull one of his guns out of action. Although it is not mentioned in the

Official History, this Officer's account makes it clear that something near a panic had occurred in the vicinity of Bur-corps' Headquarters, some ten miles north of Alon. In any event, Headquarters Bur-corps Cipher Staff lost their re-ciphering tables and these were never recovered. For-tunately, these tables were what were known as the 'Pagoda Tables' and were only used for India–Burma traffic and, therefore, no great harm was done.

In view of the Officers' reassurances, I decided that we should return to our village and trusted that we should be able to spend the rest of the night in bed. This wish was not fulfilled for, shortly after our return, a messenger arrived from Shwebo with orders from General Alexander that a general retreat to India was planned. Army Headquarters would not now be coming to the village but would start moving towards India. My orders were to pack up and move back through Ye U immediately, and await Army Head-quarters a few miles up the track to India.

Everyone was aroused and with much cursing and grous-ing, we got on the road back to Ye U. Ye U, itself, was in a state of panic – lights everywhere, lorries being loaded frantically and people running aimlessly here and there. In the middle of this chaos I saw a company of the Burma Military Police standing quietly and steadily on parade. The Officer Commanding was Peter Hoole, an Assistant Super-intendent in the Burma Police, who had done sterling work as an Officer of the Rangoon Police during the evacuation period. I asked him what he was doing and I received the laconic reply: 'I can't do anything in the dark so I am going to dismiss my men until it is light and I can see what I am doing.'

My orders, however, were to proceed up the Kalewa track. It was pitch dark and before long I had not the least idea of where I was or how far I had gone, and to make matters worse I could find no trace of the rest of Headquarters so after searching about for a while longer without success, I decided it would be wiser to stop where I was until dawn. At this point a reserve officer of the Royal Marines loomed out of the night. He was originally part of the Intelligence staff when Army Headquarters had had a coast line to look after; he started a long tirade about my having received orders to meet Army Headquarters and that there was nothing for me to do but meet Army Headquarters. I replied curtly that it was dark, I had no idea where I was, I was tired and in any case I was in command. This being so I proposed to bed down in the car and would deal with all problems in the morning.

This particular Royal Marine Officer had had a sore disappointment earlier. He had remained with Army Headquarters after the fall of Rangoon, as there was nowhere else for him to go, and when a call came for volunteers with ship experience to help the Irrawaddy Flotilla Company this seemed a godsend to him. He set off for Mandalay fully expecting to be given command of a ship and returned shortly after having been told that he was too old to stoke the boilers.

I was just settling down to try to get some sleep when another minor panic occurred. A curious rumbling sound obtruded itself on our consciousness and many thought it was the noise of Japanese tanks but mercifully it proved to be no more than the rush of water over the weirs of an irrigation canal. At long last I was able to curl up on the back seat of the car and sleep for the short time remaining before the dawn.

The next morning we heard that the Army Commander and the remainder of Army Headquarters would be arriving shortly and we settled down at the side of the road to await them. In the interim a motley throng passed us, the poor wretched 'useless mouths' whom circumstances had now forced to make their way to India on foot; among them, somewhat to our amusement, were Widdicombe and Gates, both in vile tempers at being deprived of their relatively comfortable steamer trip up the Chindwin. Our two security prisoners also appeared, moving unescorted, towards India. They had been sent off from Shwebo in the charge of some

British Regimental Police from the Shwebo Transit Camp. In the confusion caused by the panic at Alon, they had lost their captors but they obviously considered the British a better risk than the Japanese and willingly joined the other refugees.

The Official History states that General Alexander met General Stilwell at Ye U on the evening of 1st May and it was decided that the withdrawal from the Irrawaddy line should take place without delay. According to the orders I received at about 1 a.m. on that day, it appears that General Alexander must have made up his mind to this at least 24 hours earlier. I clearly remember the messenger saying: 'We are off up the road!' – meaning the road to India.

VII

Return to India

We started our retreat to India on the arrival of the remainder of Army Headquarters, when we all moved up the Kalewa track together; our first halt came in the vicinity of Kaduma and with it came the full realisation of the magnitude of the task of withdrawing the Army to India. The track, on which the whole of the British withdrawal depended, was narrow, sandy and included a difficult hill section involving several hairpin bends, steep gradients and flimsy bridges. General Alexander is reported to have said that it was difficult to imagine how a force with motor transport could have passed over it all.

Ye U to the Chindwin at Shwegyin was a distance of about 100 miles and from Shwegyin onwards to Klaing, near Kalewa on the opposite bank, there was a track suitable for refugees on foot but not for fully equipped infantry or transport. The great bulk of the force, therefore, had to be transported from Shwegyin some six or seven miles up river and landed on the opposite bank at Kalewa. From Kalewa to near Kalemyo, there was a good metalled road and after that another track led to Tamu, about 70 miles north up the Kabaw Valley. This track was, in general, in better condition than the one to Shwegyin as, being nearer to India, it had received the attentions of the engineers who, at the beginning of the year, had started to convert the whole section Tamu–Ye U into a motor road. From Tamu onwards a fairly reasonable road went over the mountains to Palel in India. The big bottleneck was the river crossing; six steamers were available, each having the capacity to take about 600 men but only two lorries and two jeeps each, and to make matters worse there was no jetty at Shwegyin – at least not until a makeshift one was constructed by the Sappers. Unfortunately, due probably to pre-monsoon storms, the river level rose before the final evacuation, effectively bringing to a halt the ferrying across of further vehicles.

The whole of Bur-corps had to come up this track, except for the 2nd Burma Brigade which had been sent to Kalemyo by the 'back door' of the Myittha Valley, plus a rapidly disintegrating number of base and line of communication units, thousands of civilian refugees, and, owing to the cessation of casualty evacuation by air, a large number of wounded, estimated at about 2,300. The fact that the majority of this vast horde reached safety must be credited to the superhuman efforts of the Administrative and Line of Communication Staff led by the Major-General Administration of Burma Army, 'Eric' Goddard and the Line of Communication Commander, my old Instructor of the Command Intelligence Course, now Major-General A. V. T. Wakeley. They had provided staging camps at intervals along the track, with dumps of food, medical posts, etc., for both military personnel and civilians.

On the other side of the Chindwin, thanks to the direct link with India, Headquarters IV Corps, which had been hurried up to Imphal, had put down similar dumps and was responsible for our reception, if and when we reached India. This assistance was of the greatest value but India could not spare any troops, except by denuding the defences which were being hastily constructed on her border – Burma Army had to get out by its own efforts.

It is understandable that those who suffered worst during this part of the retreat, were the refugees, included among whom were the civilian element of the 'useless mouths', and the wounded. General Alexander, to his eternal credit, had

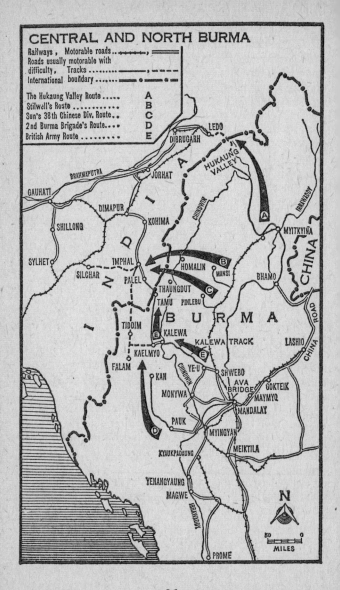

CENTRAL AND NORTH BURMA

Railways , Motorable roads ...., ═══
Roads usually motorable with
difficulty , Tracks ══════, ─────
International boundary ......• •

The Hukaung Valley Route .....   A
Stilwell's Route ....   B
Sun's 38th Chinese Div. Route..   C
2nd Burma Brigade's Route....   D
British Army Route ....   E

LEDO
DIBRUGARH
HUKAUNG VALLEY
A
BRAHMAPUTRA
JORHAT
I N D I A
CHINDWIN
IRRAWADDY
GAUHATI
DIMAPUR
KOHIMA
MYITKYINA
SHILLONG
CHINA
SYLHET
IMPHAL
HOMALIN
B
MANSI
BHAMO
SILCHAR
PALEL
C
THAUNGDUT
TAMU PINLEBU
I N D I A
TIDDIM
B U R M A
KALEWA
E
KALEWA TRACK
LASHIO
KAELMYO
E
CHINA ROAD
FALAM
YE-U
SHWEBO
KAN
AVA BRIDGE
GOKTEIK
MONYWA
MAYMYO
MANDALAY
PAUK
MYINGYAN
D
KYAUKPADAUNG
MEIKTILA
YENANGYAUNG
MAGWE
IRRAWADDY
N
50   0
MILES
PROME

agreed that the Army must accept responsibility for feeding the refugees and that, where possible, they should be lifted in military transport. To this end he had personally ordered Ramamirthan to go amongst the refugees in the camps, see that they were receiving rations and, while possible, load them into lorries. Many refugees owed their lives to this policy and to Ramamirthan's energy. The plight of the wounded was dreadful; originally they had been evacuated by air from Shwebo and when this airfield had been put out of action, sent by train to Myitkyina for air evacuation. These two routes were comparatively short and comfortable but now, with the airfields gone, they had to be taken up the track in ambulances or even in such transport as could be improvised. The jolting of the vehicles due to the execrable surface of the track and the time taken to bring them to Shwegyin, there to be loaded on to the ferry and off again for a further journey by road to Imphal must have added greatly to the suffering of the more lightly wounded and been almost unendurable for those who were severely wounded, especially as the whole journey took between four and five days. In addition, during the whole of this time, except for the crossing of the river, they could not even be taken off the ambulances. The most the medical detachment could do, on arrival at an overnight staging post, was to make them as comfortable as possible without even being able to take them off their stretchers.

At our first camp after leaving Ye U, I was giving orders to go forward and see how things were progressing and, in particular, to note how the transport was coping with the hill section. A number of expert British drivers from the Armoured Brigade had been stationed here in order to take over the vehicles from the regular drivers and bring them through the section. I happened to arrive when a convoy of ambulances was going through and I shall never be able to erase from my memory the agony of the wounded and the stench from their hastily applied dressings which could not be changed except in an extreme emergency, all of which was aggravated by the tropical heat, which itself was at its worst as it was immediately prior to the onset of the monsoon.

The retreat had now become a race against the weather and the Japanese. We were into May, the month in which the monsoon breaks in that part of Burma and, once the torrential rains started, all vehicular movement on any unmetalled road would be forced to come to a halt. The odds in favour of the Japanese were strengthened in that the loss of Monwya meant that we could no longer move troops on both sides of the Chindwin and the river route therefore was open to them. Not only could they drive ahead to Kalewa but in many places routes following water courses ran laterally from the Chindwin to cut across the Shwegyin track. An attempt was made to block this flank threat by using the composite British Battalion; unfortunately on one occasion they misunderstood their orders and retreated precipitately, involving a company of the 7th Gurkhas. One result of this was that the Company Commander of the Gurkhas was drowned while trying to swim the Chindwin, after he found himself surrounded by the Japanese.

After a day or so at our first camp, Headquarters moved on to Pyingaing, rather over half-way to Shwegyin. On arrival we made ourselves comfortable in the village houses, but, owing to the threat of a Japanese sneak attack from the Chindwin, we had to spend the night in our cars 'lagered' in some fields nearby. The next day I was given a new job. General Alexander ordered me to take a party up the road to a point about 6 miles from Shwegyin in order to establish a road block to prevent transport proceeding indiscriminately to the ferry. The river had risen and submerged the jetty and while the Sappers had hopes of reconstructing it, at that time no vehicles could be got on to the steamers. To prevent congestion near the jetty only four-wheeled drive unit vehicles and ambulances were to be allowed past the road block. All load carrying transport (3-tonners) were to be turned round and sent back to run a shuttle service to bring on unattached military personnel and civilian refugees. This was going to be a difficult operation as, by now, most lorries had become separated from their officers and transport units had become very mixed up and, naturally enough, the drivers were anxious to regain their units and reluctant to go back in the direction of the enemy. However my orders were unequivocal: no exceptions were to be made, nor any excuses accepted and as a last resort I had been given plenary powers to shoot anyone who disobeyed orders. Fortunately most drivers were co-operative and even the exceptions succumbed to persuasion, so that nothing worse than a few heated arguments occurred.

It soon became apparent that a fair number of vehicles, both military and civilian, would accumulate at the road block and that these would have to be denied to the enemy. A tank from the Armoured Brigade, together with its British crew, was allotted to smash up these vehicles and every so often it would charge into a group of vehicles and render them unfit for further use. A party of the Governor's staff appeared in the Governor's official Rolls-Royce and this set the tank crew quite a problem, for although they charged it time and again, it resisted their efforts amazingly well but at last it was immolated – a tribute to British workmanship.

We suffered some annoyance from a Japanese fixed under-carriage plane which every now and again machine gunned our position. I well remember moving cautiously round a tree, keeping the trunk between me and the Jap. Except for this it was peaceful enough but it was heartrending to see the stream of humanity which flowed past us – men, women and children, of all ages – all moving on as best they could towards their goal, India. At last the rear echelons of the fighting brigades began to arrive and it was time to continue our journey. The Japanese had by now started to bomb the ferry steamers, with the obvious result that the crews were refusing to work except at night and, therefore, I thought it only prudent to organise our departure so that we should arrive at the ferry about dusk.

My poor old mudplastered Ford V8, which had brought us safely from Rangoon, had to be destroyed by the tank and the problem now was, what should Sergeant Rivers and I carry with us. Army Headquarters had gone ahead and we were faced with the prospect of a long walk, so we had to carry what comforts we could while still keeping the load light. We each took a pack containing such necessaries as a change of underclothes, razor, knife, fork and mess tin and most important of all, a mosquito net; I had, in addition, a pewter tankard attached to my belt in lieu of the more usual tin mug. We also had with us a sack of tinned rations which we carried slung on a bamboo, coolie fashion, that is, we each took an end of the bamboo on our shoulder with the load hanging between us. The only luxury which I still possessed was the better part of a bottle of whisky. We joined the queue at the jetty and eventually got on board, although the wait was shorter than we had anticipated it would be. As the steamer forged upstream towards Kalewa, I said to Rivers, 'Let's drink a toast – farewell to Burma!' He, nothing loath, agreed and finding a piece of string, I tied it to my tankard and then fished up some river water and in due course, having added the necessary tots, we drank our toast. The river water was not exactly pure but we trusted that the whisky would effectively deal with any foreign bodies, or germs.

The steamer duly arrived at Kalewa and to my great joy I spied Tony Summersell on the jetty – if he had managed to get his truck across, we should be spared any further walking – and at that moment Fate decided to deal me a blow. I gave my pack a hitch as I moved on to the gang-plank and my precious bottle of whisky shot out of the top and was lost in the river; that farewell drink proved to be more prophetic than I had realised and was certainly going to be my last one for many a long day. Muttering imprecations I proceeded towards the shore and was greeted by Tony with the good news that he had, in fact, got his truck and that Army Headquarters was only about one hour's drive away. He took us to a transit camp for the night and there I met 'Porky' Ewens who, like me, had been given a special job to do, but I never heard what it had involved; what I did hear, some weeks later, was that he had died of a ruptured appendix only a day or so after that night.

Burma Army Headquarters were established in a bungalow which belonged to one of the British timber firms and was situated a few miles up the track towards Tamu. The main feature of the place was the large number of enormous tree trunks which littered the ground surrounding the bungalow. The tempers of those already there were a little frayed, to put it mildly, for the Japanese had just carried out one of many raids and although casualties were very light, everyone was on edge. The reason that the casualties were light appeared to be that in the absence of slit trenches, all had flung themselves down in the lee of or between the tree trunks; all that is except General Alexander himself, who had remained upright and as always, completely imperturbable but even he, like the rest, was very angry.

I was told that the Japanese had been raiding Headquarters not only every day but also several times each day and the General was convinced that the close proximity of the Headquarters unit of the Burmese Army Signals was to blame – either someone was giving our position away or else the Japanese were using D/F equipment to pin-point the site. The Signals unit was one of the newly raised technical units of the Burma Army and contained a high proportion of well educated Burmans, whose morale and loyalty was an unknown quantity. In general the Burmese units had behaved extremely well throughout and the other battalions of the Burma Rifles, in which Kachins, Chins and Kerens predominated, had fought magnificently and the same could be said of the Burma Frontier Force. The Burma Military Police had not taken part in active operations to the same extent but they, too, had stood up well to the ordeal of the retreat.

The steadiness displayed by Peter Hoole's Company in

Ye U on the night of 30th April was beyond all praise, especially when compared with the panic all around them. Now, however, the situation was changing because the British were nearly out of Burma and the ties of family began to loom large in the minds of the Burmese soldiers. A steady trickle of desertions began as units neared the Chindwin; Summersell had told me that his Kachin Havildar had quietly slipped away on arrival at Kalewa. The Army Commander now decided that it was too much to demand of the Burmese troops that they leave their families to their fate and so a general authorisation was given to discharge, honourably, any soldier who desired to return to his home. The majority took advantage of this but still a sizeable number, mostly single men, did decide to come through to India where, after reorganisation, they did very well particularly in operations where local knowledge was at a premium, such as Wingate's Chindit operations.

Control of the Chin Hills District having been retained by the British, the local Battalion of the Burma Frontier Force remained in being and the establishment of a post at Fort Hertz, by the end of the monsoon, led to the raising of local forces in the area. These were known as the Kachin Levies. In the Field Security Sections out of the three or four Burmese 'ranks', one Naik, Saw William, a Christian Karen came out with us. At a later date he went through the Field Security Course at the Intelligence School, Karachi, and returned as a Havildar to a section under my control in Assam, where his intelligence and westernised behaviour led him to be generally known as Sergeant Williams.

By the time Army Headquarters had reached Kalewa, the old peace-time establishment of officers and clerks normally totalling a hundred or more, had shrunk to a mere handful. On the General Staff side, after the Army Commander himself, there was the Major-General, General Staff – Major-General Winterton, who was a personal appointment of General Alexander and two GSO IIs (Operations) – Major Crowther of the 60th Rifles and a younger brother of

Lieutenant-General Montgomery, later Field Marshal Montgomery of Alamein, Major Montgomery of the Baluch Regiment of the Indian Army. In Intelligence we had the GSO I – Philip Gwyn; the GSO III I(a), myself – GSO II I(b), the GSO III I(b) – Bill Talbot, and some four or five Intelligence Officers. The Administrative Staff was down to two, the Major-General Administration – Eric Goddard, and one staff officer. The total officer strength was in the region of 15 to 20 persons. Such luxuries as Mess units, employment or guard platoons were non-existent; the handful of Field Security of No. 1 Section were our only protection, and for our creature comforts there was a motley collection of civilian mess and private servants under the control of an elderly Sergeant of the Burma Auxiliary Force. He prepared our meals and we had to line up with our mugs and mess tins to collect them; the meals never varied – boiled rice and tinned sausages and not very much of either – all washed down with tea.

This attenuated Headquarters could now be moved in about three 3-tonners, if one excluded the very senior officers who had their own transport. Coincidental with my arrival was the arrival of three 3-tonners, with British drivers, which had been sent from India by Headquarters IV Corps. The Army Commander decided that we should move to Tamu forthwith and that I should command the move. I was instructed to take the three 3-tonners and, on arrival at Tamu, to go about three miles down the track to Sittaung and establish Headquarters in a jungle village. At the same time Burma Army Headquarters Signals were told to go about three miles from Tamu, in a different direction, so that a sizeable distance would separate us and lessen the risk of their presence giving us away. I had hardly moved off from our log-strewn location when our poor old Headquarters received yet another pasting from the air.

We settled into our village near Tamu and spent about a week there, in comparative peace. There was little work to do as the detailed direction of the withdrawal was with Headquarters Bur-corps. General Alexander, very properly, considered that he should not leave Burma until he was certain that all troops were safely over the Chindwin. This led to the curious situation where General Slim and his Headquarters were back in India, at Palel, while Army Headquarters was still at Tamu, and towards the end, it was nearer to the front line than was healthy.

Anti-aircraft precautions were carried out with great care after our previous experiences with Japanese bombers. Early every morning we went out to a nearby stream where we washed, shaved and laundered our clothes but as soon as the sun was well up everyone had to be back in his village hut; all transport was under cover and all outside movement was kept to the minimum. We escaped any bombing, although Japanese planes were seen daily but whether it was as a result of the restriction of movement or because of the removal of the Burma Army Signals was never ascertained. Under these conditions the days passed very slowly and we all longed to be able to return to civilisation. Philip Gwyn left Tamu shortly after our arrival in order to report on the situation to Headquarters IV Corps and for a short while I became the senior Intelligence Officer.

It was during this period that we were visited by a party of journalists, notably Marsland Gander and Alfred Wagg. They had flown out of Burma and had now returned, by road, from India. The GSO III I(a) laid on a press conference and I told him that, at all costs, he was to get us a bottle of whisky as we had all been 'dry' for far too long – in my case, ever since I lost my bottle at the Chindwin. He was inclined to emphasise the difficulties of granting my request but I persisted, pointing out that the correspondents having come from Calcutta, were probably loaded with the stuff. However, he overcame his scruples and later on when the correspondents had left, we were able to celebrate their visit with a tot of Haig all round.

The race for Shwegyin continued but fortunately was finally won by the British by a very short head indeed. The

Japanese arrived at the ferry while Headquarters 17th Indian Division, the 48th (all Gurkha) Indian Brigade, who were acting as rearguard, together with the garrison of Shwegyin, were still on the wrong side of the river. Although these troops put up a good fight against mounting Japanese pressure, it became impossible to embark any further personnel, as the jetty was under fire and the flotilla of river steamers had disintegrated. The remaining British forces, therefore, had to move up the track to Klaing, opposite Kalewa, and luckily the enemy did not pursue, for movement was very slow owing to the badness of the track and the congestion on it. Everyone arrived at Kalewa by the evening of 11th May, where the 48th Indian Brigade and one British Regiment embarked to sail up river direct to Sittaung, and arrived there on 14th May. The first heavy rain of the monsoon fell on 12th May, making the retreat a very close run thing indeed.

The Chinese Armies, at this period, were moving northwards towards Myitkyina, covered by Sun's 38th Division but before they could establish themselves there, the Japanese moving swiftly from Bhamo, captured it first. The Chinese forces then broke up, one division managing to by-pass Myitkyina reached Yunnan by way of Fort Hertz, another moved on India by the incredibly difficult route up the Hukawng Valley; they did not arrive in Assam until the end of July. Sun, himself, led his Division due west and after a number of spirited actions against the enemy, duly arrived in Imphal.

We received our marching orders on about 15th May and moved back over the mountain range to the Indian native state of Manipur where, on 20th May, operational command passed to IV Corps and Burma Army, as an operational formation, ceased to exist. A number of us were sent to a Government Rest House at Kanglatongbi, a few miles north of Imphal and where the main road to India proper, left the Manipur plain and plunged into the Naga Hills on its long and tortuous passage to the railhead at Dimapur. Here we were told to await further orders.

The reception arrangements for Burma Army on their arrival in India must be commented upon for they were considerably less than adequate. Units or individuals were directed to camps or camping sites and beyond the issue of rations and a very limited issue of clothing, little else was done for the time being. No blame can be attached to any individual for this state of affairs, it simply arose from the general unpreparedness of India to fight a war on its own territory. In the first winter of the war, India had sent a force to the Middle East and within her own borders had constructed a series of defences in the North West Frontier Province against a possible Russian attack through Afghanistan. In 1941 further and considerable Indian forces were sent to the Middle East and later in the year to Malaya and Burma; the result of this great effort was that by May 1942, the forces existing within India were quite inadequate to defend the country from a Japanese attack, contain the local tribesmen on the North West Frontier and provide forces for Internal Security; in fact, the forces on the entire Burma frontier comprised no more than nine Brigades, and much of this force was still moving up to its frontier positions.

However, this was not the whole of the story; the pre-1939 mobilisation plans for India had envisaged a defence of the North West Frontier, and the bulk of the depots, concentration areas and cantonments had been here, with good roads and railways ready to move up and supply a force in this part of India. Now everything had to be turned about and sent up into a relatively backward north-east, where road communications were poor, the railways were of metre gauge, necessitating a break of gauge transhipment and both road and rail were interrupted by the great unbridged river line of the Brahmaputra, over which there were only few and indifferent road and rail ferries. By April, the chaos and congestion on the railways was such that Wavell was reporting to London that it took seven weeks to move a Brigade from Ranchi, east of Calcutta, to the Assam frontier, a journey which, in normal times, would have taken an individual between 36 and 48 hours.

It was obvious to those in authority that only the essentials to maintain the forces which had been hastily sent to the border and to sustain life in the remnants of Burma Army could be got up and there was literally no capacity for any comforts. None of this was obvious to Burma Army and naturally resentment became widespread. The natural cohesion of the fighting units sustained their morale but for the others herded into improvised camps in the Manipur plain, morale was at a very low ebb. Added to this was the unfortunate fact that Headquarters IV Corps was a British Army unit newly arrived from England, with a provost unit of tough and efficient British military policemen with no experience of Indian troops; on the other hand, Indian troops had, until now, no experience of British MPs. In pre-war days provost work was done by Regimental and Garrison Police, British and Indians dealing with their own kind. Base and transport unit personnel, whose units had, through circumstances and no fault of their own, disintegrated at the Chindwin crossing, now found themselves treated by the British MPs as, at the best, stragglers, and at the worst, deserters and these men became both bewildered and resentful, not without reason.

Owing to the shortage of arms, an order was given that all officers must give up their revolvers and a party of Military Police at Dimapur station rigidly enforced this. Most officers were very bitter at this order, particularly Regular Officers whose revolvers were their personal property. I heard of this order and luckily, having my Walther instead of a service revolver, was able to keep it in my pocket and thus evade the prying eyes of MPs.

The first day our party spent at Kanglatongbi was passed in trying to obtain some clothing from a nearby Ordnance Depot but we were rebuffed on the grounds that officers were not entitled to free clothing and such things as 'Officers' Shops' were still unknown in India. On the following day we were becoming desperate and hearing that there was a bulk canteen at Dimapur or Manipur Road, as the railway station at Dimapur was called, we clubbed together and taking all the money we could lay our hands on, another officer and I set off on the long and tedious drive over the mountains to Dimapur. We 'borrowed' a 3-tonner and an Indian driver and left at dusk, but, owing to a breakdown and innumerable delays to let convoys through in the opposite direction, we did not arrive there until about noon on the following day. On arrival we were told, much to our annoyance and consternation, that no south-bound traffic would be allowed to leave after 1 p.m. This would hardly have given us time to get our canteen stores, load up and get back to the control gate so I went to the Base Headquarters Office to get a special authorisation. By great good fortune, the officer concerned was an old friend of mine, Philip Panton of the 2nd Gurkhas, and although at first he refused us permission, he eventually agreed to give us thirty minutes' grace.

Our purchases at the Base Canteen did not take long but, as we were about to pay, trouble arose; from the earliest times of British rule, Indian currency was also the currency of Burma, but, from the separation in 1937, although the coins remained the same, special notes for use only in Burma were issued by the Reserve Bank of India from its Rangoon branch. These notes were distinguished by having their numbers in red and, of course, these were the notes we preferred to pay for our purchases. An extremely unpleasant officer in charge refused to take our money and when we protested, said it could be changed by the Field Cashier but he, at that time, was absent. In view of Philip Panton's very definite instructions that we only had thirty minutes' grace at the control gate, it was quite impossible for us to await the return of the Field Cashier and get away that day.

Impasse. We had taken the 3-tonner and left without any real authority and were, therefore, desperately anxious not to be away any longer than was absolutely necessary. We had so nearly succeeded in achieving our object that I for one was in a mental state that would brook no further hindrance. I was determined to get those stores which included toothbrushes, toothpaste, razor blades and such like articles – vital necessities to those of us who had not seen a shop or a canteen for at least two months. In fact my determination was such that I was on the point of drawing my pistol and taking the stores by force (an act which could well have had the direst consequences for me), when the canteen's British Warrant Officer said, 'Don't worry, Sir, pay me and I will see that the money is changed.' This surprising over-ruling of his orders seemed to satisfy the Officer in Charge and, thankfully, we loaded up and set off southwards to Kanglatongbi which we reached late in the evening after a speedy and uneventful run.

Once again a surprise awaited me. Orders had come in that I and a number of other officers were to leave the following morning on ten days' refitting leave, prior to joining IV Corps Headquarters – it was a case of Dimapur here we come – again!

VIII

Civilisation Again

We arrived back in Dimapur in the evening and were put up for the night in a transit camp, with an attendant lack of comforts. Our party consisted of Philip Gwyn, about four or five others and myself, together with those servants who had remained faithful to us in spite of all that had happened. Manuel was one of these and he was looking forward with pleasure to returning to his native Madras but, unfortunately for him, he contracted a bout of fever at Dimapur. However, nothing could persuade him to consent to being left behind in the wilds of Assam so, heavily dosed with aspirin, he continued to accompany us.

We had two 'Type X' enciphering machines and two boxes of cipher books with us and these items were, at one and the same time, the source of great satisfaction and also great irritation to us. The satisfaction was occasioned by the fact that these machines speeded up signal traffic enormously and, as they were in very short supply in the East, they were literally 'worth their weight in gold' to the Army. The irritation was that they had to be guarded and often man-handled by us – these machines and books were contained in four extremely heavy and bulky packing cases, which gives an idea of the problem.

I had no definite idea of how or where I should spend my refitting leave. At that time I had no home in India, other than my Regiment, and so I decided to go to the Regimental Depot at Dehra Dun, in spite of the fact that it would involve a journey of at least three days either way. The local Headquarters issued us with 1st class travel warrants but, in view of the prevailing conditions, this was not the type of accommodation we travelled in for the early part of our journey. There were normally two trains a day proceeding in the right direction, an all stations 'passenger' and the 'Mail'. The latter connected at the Brahmaputra ferry with the metre gauge Mail on the other side, which in turn connected with the broad gauge Mail to Calcutta. The Mail left Manipur Road (Dimapur) in the morning of Day 1, according to the time table, dinner being taken on the ferry. The second metre gauge Mail connected, in the morning of Day 2, with the broad gauge train which finally arrived at Calcutta that evening – a journey of about 32 hours.

We had heard that owing to the disorganisation, no real time table was being kept to, at least not on our side of the Brahmaputra and we should be well advised to get on the first train available. Immediately after breakfast we went to the station and found the 'passenger' standing there. The accommodation, of all classes, was already full but at the rear there was a four-wheeled parcel van and this we commandeered. It was fitted with wooden shelves, which, although hard, would allow us to lie down. It had no refinements such as a fan but it did have electric light. We were hailed in a very loud American accent, shortly before departure, and upon enquiry as to the reason for this, discovered that the War Correspondent Alfred Wagg was desirous of joining our party. At first we did not greet this idea with any great enthusiasm, in view of our cargo of cipher machines and books but, finally, we agreed to take him. It was just as well that we did because 'Waggie', as we came to know him, had with him a large stock of food whereas we had none. In normal times meals could be obtained at railway refreshment rooms but on this section, at this stage, late running and overcrowding had played havoc with this service. A fact which our journey did nothing to disprove.

We left Manipur Road at about 10 a.m. and had only made the next station when we were held up for some five hours owing to a breakdown ahead. The next station with a refreshment room was not reached until after dark. Thanks to Waggie we, at least, were well fed and relatively comfortable. On the evening of the second day we eventually reach Gauhati, the town near where the ferry was situated, and here further trouble arose. The railway authorities on the other bank of the Brahmaputra were under a different administration, being of the Eastern Bengal Railway, and had given up trying to make connections with our side, which was under the administration of the Assam Bengal Railway.

Our train was now almost exactly on the time of the Assam Bengal Mail and, if it moved forward to the ferry station, would be in time to catch both the ferry and the Eastern Bengal Mail. The authorities at Gauhati, knowing that their Mail train was only one station behind, wished, rather naturally, to side track us and send the Mail through to make the connection. It could not be said that this was a normal connection as the Mail was almost exactly 24 hours late and our train was about 36 hours late. Should the Mail be sent ahead, we could say goodbye to arriving at Calcutta on the following day and would have to spend at least the next 24 hours hanging about Gauhati. A furious altercation broke out on the platform between officers from our train and the railway staff. The final outcome resulted in our moving on, to our great joy and relief.

We dined on the ferry and found the Eastern Bengal Mail awaiting us on the farther side. We were able to obtain one first class berth which was given to Philip Gwyn by virtue of his seniority, and one intermediate class compartment originally designed to seat about twenty people, which allowed plenty of room for us all to lie down, as well as space for our other equipment. We arrived at the break of gauge station before breakfast the next morning and to our relief, the broad gauge Mail was waiting on the other platform – a corridor train with a Restaurant Car; one of the very few running in India at that time. Waggie told us to take our time in transferring our gear, as he would get seats for us in the Restaurant Car. We got our kit over and deposited it in our new compartment therefore, before going in search of breakfast. In due course we found Waggie presiding over our table, which was embellished by a very welcome, though slightly unorthodox breakfast beverage – an open bottle of beer by each place. Calcutta was reached that afternoon after a blissfully uneventful run and that night we slept in real beds with proper bedding, for the first time in many weeks.

On the following day, I went out to buy some very necessary clothes and then feeling more or less presentable again, I set off for Delhi by the Toofan (Whirlwind) Express. I had asked Manuel to continue in my service but he wanted to go home to Madras so, with great regret, I paid him off, gave him his ticket to Madras and something extra because he had served me extremely well during the far from pleasant period of the retreat. It seemed a rather mundane ending to what had been a period of fellowship unusual between master and man, except in times of stress.

The circumstances of the last months had done nothing to improve the physical condition of those involved and I was no exception. I had lost two stones in weight and had not realised what havoc varied and plentiful food could wreak on someone long unaccustomed to it until, just as the train was nearing Delhi, I suddenly became very ill with severe stomach pains. These pains were so violent that I was quite unable to leave the train. Fortunately there was another officer in the compartment and he immediately telephoned to the British Military Hospital for an ambulance, when the train reached Delhi. The station is in the Old City of Delhi and the hospital was situated in the Cantonment – a distance of some twelve miles separated the two and in view of this, it took the ambulance an appreciable time to reach me.

In the intervening period a Ticket Collector visited me to find out why I had not left the train and initially he had difficulty in understanding the position. He kept repeating parrot fashion, 'It is against rule and regulation of railway for passengers to remain in train when it is going to siding.' Eventually, however, my explanations penetrated through to his understanding and he said with great emphasis, 'You are ill!' Satisfied on this point and on being reassured that an ambulance was on the way, he left me in peace. The train was then shunted on to the carriage sidings. There I stayed for what seemed an eternity until, at last, I heard the crunch of boots on the ballast and a cheery voice shouting, 'Where are you, Sir?' I directed the caller and soon two British Orderlies of the RAMC appeared, put me on a stretcher and before long I was in hospital, starting on the road to recovery – the 'Great Retreat' was over for me.

I was discharged from hospital after a week's stay. The medical authorities wished to put me before a Medical Board to assess what sick leave I should be granted. This I resisted strongly as, in all probability, it would have prejudiced my chances of taking up my new job in Assam. The doctors saw my point of view and agreed that if I were to be granted a month's ordinary leave, they would discharge me without a Medical Board. The Intelligence Branch at Army Headquarters gave me this leave without demur and ordered me to report back to Assam at its termination. I spent an enjoyable month, partly in my Regimental Centre at Dehra Dun and partly in the adjacent hill station of Mussoorie.

It is easy to be wise after the event but my well intentioned keenness had an unfortunate effect on my career. I learned, subsequently, that while I was on leave the Intelligence School had asked for me to take up the new joint appointment of Chief Instructor Field Security Wing and Commandant Intelligence Corps (India) with the rank of Lieutenant-Colonel. In addition to this, the Commandant of the newly raised 5th Battalion of my Regiment had asked for me as Second in Command; both these appointments would have led to higher appointments. Had I been on sick leave, I should have been borne on the books of my Regimental Centre as a reinforcement available for posting but on ordinary leave I was, in fact, a GSO II of Headquarters IV Corps and they, faced with the formidable task of securing the eastern frontier with very inadequate resources, flatly refused to release me so, at the end of my leave, it was back to Assam and IV Corps. They could not be blamed for their attitude as they had a difficult job to do and not unnaturally wished to retain everyone allotted to them. Even before I had left Manipur for my leave, the Commander IV Corps, Lieutenant-General N. M. S. Irwin, had issued a statement, part of which read, ' . . . the resources of my corps are inadequate to meet the many demands placed on it by the circumstances of the arrival of the Burma Army and by the flow of refugees, and it therefore will be necessary, as it has been already, to retain the services of certain officers and other ranks and units forming part of corps and army troops to assist in the reorganising of the divisions.' This obviously referred to the necessity for retaining all Intelligence and Security officers and that meant me, along with the rest.

The monsoon, which had so effectively stopped the Japanese advance, had had less satisfactory repercussions within India; the whole of the metre gauge railway line along the north bank of the Brahmaputra was washed out, necessitating a long detour by rail and steamer and then rail again before I could reach Gauhati and my new appointment.

My new job was to organise security in the rear areas of IV Corps and I was ordered to set up a semi-independent organisation in Gauhati, to be known as the Gauhati Intelligence Detachment, but which was an integral part of Headquarters IV Corps. The local Commander in Gauhati was General 'Eric' Goddard, late MGA Burma Army.

Troops and stores were pouring into Assam and units of the Burma Army and of the Chinese Armies were flooding out and, as might be expected, chaos prevailed. Once again we were faced with the problem of an absence of identity cards, a total lack of security training and few security units. My own staff consisted of the original GSO III of IV Corps, Peter Leefe of the Intelligence Corps, British Army, a very experienced Security Officer who had been a Sergeant in one of the original British Field Security Sections in France in 1939–40 and 'Rama' Ramamirthan. The total Field Security resources in Assam were two sections only – the IV Corps Section, a highly trained all British Section which had come from England with the Corps Headquarters and an all Indian Section newly raised at Karachi which was at Manipur Road and doing nothing because the Commanding Officer had been evacuated as a mental case. We did not consider that these two Sections were of value as they stood so we broke them up and made two composite sections; in addition there were a number of men – British an Indian – of the Burma Sections. We adopted the same policy as in Burma, that was, the fighting troops could look after themselves but the great mass of administrative units now coming into the Assam Valley required as full a security cover as could be impro-vised. A section was placed at Manipur Road and another at Dibrugarh in North Assam and a detachment at Gauhati.

I remained in Assam for well over a year but the events of most of that period are irrelevant to this book but what is relevant are the problems caused by the fresh influx of refugees which began again at the end of the monsoon, that is in October, and which was linked to the original retreat.

We were still grappling with the organisation of security in the area when, in about October, orders were received that refugee camps were to be set up with the object of screening these unfortunate people now arriving in India. Those who arrived with the army in May had dispersed without any check and having been ahead of the Japanese invasion could hardly be expected to have been infiltrated by spies or saboteurs. Now the situation was different; the pres-ent refugees had spent some four months or so within Burma after the British forces had left and it was no longer desirable to allow them to disperse at will. A number of agencies were involved in the operation – the local Army Headquarters – No. 202 Line of Communication Area, the Assam Police and Magistracy, the Military Police and the Intelligence organisation. 202 Area built the camps, the Civil Police guarded them, Magistrates passed detention orders as required, the Military Police and Field Security helped the Civil Police in directing refugees to the camps, and the Intelligence organisation at Army Headquarters at Delhi provided the interpreters and interrogators. The Gauhati Intelligence Detachment acted as co-ordinator for the whole operation.

The theory of the operation was excellent but before one could interrogate a refugee one had first to find him. This was a headache as the refugees naturally wished to disperse to their native areas where, in all probability, they had relatives who would care for them. We were assisted by two factors. The first was money: the Government of India had decreed that no bank should change any of the 'red numbered' bank notes valid only in Burma, without an authorisation from one of our Interrogation Camp Headquarters. This was a powerful incentive to channel the refugees into the camps but the labour involved in listing all such notes and checking them against a black list and finally issuing the clearance certificate taxed our meagre resources to the limit. The paucity of communications was the second factor; there were only two ways out of Assam and in our area was the principal one, the rail ferry at Pandu near Gauhati. Here we set up a check point physically separating by post and rails, two gangways; the one for military personnel manned by the Military Police who checked documents; the other for civilians manned by the Field Security and Assam Police.

It is obvious that in the time available no detailed questioning could take place so it was agreed that, in general, anyone who by his physical characteristics looked like a Bengali or an Assamese would be passed through. Others would be asked stock questions such as: 'Who are you?', 'Where do you work?', 'Where have you come from?'. If, for example, the man answered, 'I am a carpenter with the Assam Oil Company at Digboi,' he might then be asked, 'What time did your train leave Digboi and what is the junction nearby?' A correct answer and he passed, an incorrect one and he was put back to wait until the stream had gone through. Those put back were then questioned again and as many of them had merely panicked at the first questioning, on reflection they were able to give a clear account of themselves. They were then allowed to pass but those whose answers were still unsatisfactory, were handed over to civil police custody and removed to the camp where a magistrate passed a seven-day detention order to hold them until their *bona fides* or otherwise could be established. This was a very rough and ready method but was probably the only one possible in the circumstances. The check did produce a couple of amusing results – a Lieutenant-General who had lost his Identity Card and a civilian canteen employee with a suitcase full of stolen whisky.

In due course I left Assam with all its associations with the Great Retreat and to my eternal sorrow when, in 1944, the time came for the British Forces to return to Burma I could not be with them for I was serving on the North West Frontier with my own Regiment. Last out, first in did not apply in my case.

IX

Epilogue — Conclusions

What had been achieved – something or nothing? To quote from the Official History:

'During the campaign the Army in Burma, without once losing its cohesion, had retreated nearly one thousand miles in some three and a half months – the longest retreat ever carried out by a British Army – and for the last seven hundred miles had virtually carried its base with it.'

No retreat can be anything but a defeat, but little of this defeat can be laid to the charge of the Army in Burma. In spite of the grave defects and difficulties, the greatest, in all probability, being the complete lack of any time for rest or refit, every fighting unit arrived back in India as a formed body with every piece of equipment which could be carried, and every man, even in the base units, was in possession of his rifle or personal arm, but the losses of other equipment were heavy. All tanks and nearly all guns and vehicles, owing to the Chindwin crossing, of necessity, had been abandoned and where possible, destroyed at Shwegyin.

The praise for this remarkable feat must be given, in the first instance, to the inspired leadership of Generals Alexander and Slim and to the confidence that this inspired in all ranks, but also to the steadiness, good discipline and fighting spirit of the British, Indian and Gurkha soldiers and their Regimental Officers. Nor must the administrative staffs be forgotten, their superhuman efforts in 'carrying the base with them' had meant that while some periods we were hungry, we never starved.

All the British and Indian Field Security personnel, plus the redoubtable Naik Saw William, arrived back by various routes. Nos. 1 and 2 Sections came by the conventional route via Kalewa and Tamu, and Nos. 3 and 4 from Katha to Manipur via Homalin; the same route taken by General Stilwell and the Chinese 38th Division. Both Sections did sterling work in assisting refugees, keeping order where necessary and acting as general helpers to the overworked civil and military authorities. There is an unconfirmed report that Mansfield's Section, which was in Homalin when the civil authorities evacuated on or about 10th May, stayed on, assisting refugees, until the morning of 12th May, the day that Stilwell's party arrived. It is supposed that he had intended to stay on to meet Stilwell and assist his party but they were delayed and he and his Section moved on only a few hours before they arrived. This move out was due to a report that the Japanese had reached the Chindwin between Sittaung and Homalin. He is also supposed to have distributed to the villagers a large sum of money which had originally been given to him by the civil authorities for the assistance of refugees. The villagers were instructed that if Stilwell's party came in, they were to help them in every way in their power. Whether this actually happened is not known, but it is known that Stilwell's party arrived in the afternoon but left again at dusk and camped for the night away from the river.

We had put Field Security 'on the map' as far as the rest of the Army was concerned and it is very unfortunate that they were left out of the Order of Battle when the Official History came to be written.

The cool courage and good discipline of the four Field Security Sections was beyond praise during the whole of the campaign. In spite of the rigours, both mental and physical, of the period of the policing of Rangoon, when a crate of beer was always available in the Field Security billet for any man to help himself, no case of drunkenness or indiscipline occurred. The work of these sections was commemorated in that two sections, one of which was Summersell's, were given the title of Burma in brackets after their number, when the two remaining sections were renumbered on the Indian common roll.

The highest praise must also be given to another section of the community, namely, to those Civilian Government servants and private individuals who were caught up in the campaign, many of whom were Europeans. It has become common practice to denigrate their efforts and to paint them as stuffy, bureaucratic and inefficient but where this criticism is justified, it was due more to the system than to the individual. It should be appreciated that there had been no recruitment to the Services, nor any home leave since 1939, and the work of the Government servant had greatly increased. Many, therefore, were tired, overworked and worse still in the case of the Europeans, worried about and separated from their families.

British rule in the East had existed on the bedrock of justice and consideration for those we ruled. An Army in battle is not always gentle towards the local inhabitants and in retreat this tendency can be intensified, and the efforts made by the members of the magistracy to ensure fair play for their 'locals' was often thought of by Army Officers as deliberate obstruction. Many would have preferred to join the Armed Services but this was rigorously forbidden. Conscription of European males had been introduced in India and Burma in 1939, although the machinery was more often used to prevent Government departments and civil firms from being denuded of their executives than to force them into the Armed Services.

One other community to whom high praise is due was that of the Anglo-Indians and Anglo-Burmese; had they been formed into a military unit they would have been of little military value, yet in carrying out their normal tasks on the railways, in the Police and in similar services, they showed grit and determination and courage second to none.

In general terms it may be said that there was far more good behaviour and real courage from civilians and military alike than there were lapses from this standard. The dreadful scenes which are alleged to have occurred during the fall of Singapore were notably absent in Burma.

APPENDIX A

Civil, Military and Police Organisation in India and Burma

General

The Civil Administration of Burma, in 1942, differed from that of other parts of the then British Empire, but was in almost every respect akin to that of India, to which until 1937, it was joined. This had considerable effect on the Military organisation and readers may be confused by the various references to British Service units, Indian Army units, Burma Army units or the term Army in Burma. This Appendix is intended to give additional information to that already given in Chapter II.

Civil Administration

Burma was originally a province of India and the provincial Government was subject to the Government of India, which in its turn, was subject to the British Parliament, through the Secretary of State for India. The administration was unchanged when Burma was separated from India, except that Burma became responsible directly to the Secretary of State for those matters such as law and order, education, irrigation, etc., for which, previously, the Provincial Government had been responsible to the Government of India. In addition, Burma took over those functions previously dealt with by the Government of India such as Defence and Finance. External Affairs were always the prerogative of the British Parliament.

The senior Government officers in Burma, at the time of the transfer, belonged to the Secretary of State for India's Services, such as the Indian Civil Service, Indian Police, Indian Service of Engineers, etc.; these remained in Burma as members of the Burma Civil Service Class I, Burma Police Class I, etc., but continued to retain the privileges and conditions of their old service, and to place the letters ICS or IP after their names. All this was facilitated by the fact that the same British Minister was both Secretary of State for India and Secretary of State for Burma. The Class I Services were appointed by the Secretary of State and by 1942 the cadre was approximately 50% British and 50% Burmese with, in addition, a few Indians. The provincial Civil and Police Services which provided the lower officer ranks of the Civil Service and Police, were redesignated as Burma Civil Service Class II or Burma Police Service Class II and was locally recruited, with no Europeans in its ranks but containing a number of Anglo-Indians or Anglo-Burmese. The term Anglo-Indian or -Burmese was the legal definition of a person who was of pure European descent in the male line but was a native of India or Burma respectively. These persons were usually, but not always, of mixed blood.

The administration was unlike that of England but more akin to that of France with its 'Departments' and 'Prefets'. The country was divided into Districts and in each the District Magistrate was ultimately responsible to the Government for all services in his District. The Police were not, as in England, servants of the Law but Government servants, and were responsible to the District Magistrate for law and order in the District. In the Shan States local administration was generally in the hands of the local rulers; the measure of autonomy varying from State to State but all were subject, in the end, to the advice of the Government of Burma, as conveyed to them by the local Residents.

Military Organisation
(a) The Army in India/Burma.

This term was used to cover all land forces of the Crown in India or Burma respectively, irrespective of whether they belonged to the British Army (normally referred to the the British Service), the Indian Army or the Burma Army. The Army in India or Burma was both for operational purposes and administration autonomous, subject to the overall control of the British Parliament, through the Secretary of State.

(b) The British Service.

This comprised a number of Infantry, Cavalry and Artillery units stationed in India or Burma. These units, while remaining part of the British Army, were, during their service in these countries, not only operationally commanded but also administered, equipped and paid by them. The equipment was often on a different and lower scale than for units serving under the British War Office. It might be said that they were 'on loan' to India or Burma, and in this respect differed from British units serving in other British possessions which remained under the control of the British War Office. The British units were dependent on the Indian or Burmese Armies for their supporting arms (except Artillery) and administrative services.

(c) The Indian Army.

The Indian Army consisting, in general, of Indian soldiers and, originally, British Officers had, by 1942, a proportion of Indian Commissioned Officers. It was self-contained except for Horse and Field Artillery which, since 1861, had been provided by units of the British Royal Artillery. In Infantry and Cavalry Brigades, however, it was usual to have one British Infantry Battalion or Cavalry Regiment but by 1942 this was not general and certain Indian Brigades did not have a British unit. There were no British Warrant Officers or NCOs in Indian Infantry or Cavalry units. The only Artillery in the Indian Army, with the exception of the newly raised 1st Indian Field Regiment, were unbrigaded Mountain Artillery Batteries, normally allocated to the Indian North West Frontier. Engineer and Signal units were provided by the Indian Army, consisting of British Officers of the Royal Engineers or Royal Corps of Signals, seconded to, and soldiers of, the Indian Army. In these units there were a small number of British Warrant Officers and NCOs seconded from the British Service. In the 1st Indian Field Regiment and in the Engineer and Signal units there were, as a result of Indianisation, a few Indian Officers commissioned direct into the Indian Artillery, Indian Engineers and Indian Signals respectively.

The Services such as the Indian Army Service Corps and Indian Army Ordnance Corps also had a few British Warrant Officers, but they belonged to the Indian Army and were not seconded. No Royal Army Service Corps or Royal Army Ordnance Corps personnel normally served in India.

The Medical Services were split. British Military Hospitals were staffed by Royal Army Medical Corps personnel and Indian Military Hospitals by the Indian Medical Service. Personnel of both these Corps served in operational medical units irrespective of origin.

The Indian Army differed from the British Army in that commissioned officers did not serve below Company Second in Command. Platoons were commanded by officers promoted from the ranks; they held commissions from the Viceroy of India and not from the Sovereign and were junior to 2nd Lieutenants. The ranks were Jemadar (one star), Subedar (two stars) and Subedar Major (a crown).

The Viceroy's Commissioned Officers had no equivalent rank in the British Army. The non-commissioned ranks had separate designations:

Rank	*British equivalent*
Lance Naik	Lance Corporal
Havildar	Corporal
Naik	Sergeant

There were no Warrant Ranks in the Indian Army so a Havildar Major (equivalent to a Sergeant Major) was an appointment; the substantive rank of the holder being that of Havildar.

(d) The Burma Army.

All units in Burma were part of the Army in India until 1937 and all that has been written earlier, applied to them also. In 1937, Burma ceased to be an Independent Military District of India and became a separate Command, but this made little difference to the military setup. The British units merely passed from service 'on loan' to India to service 'on loan' to Burma. The wholly Burmese Regiment of the Indian Army, the 20th Burma Rifles became the nucleus of the Burma Army. A start was made in raising Burmese units for the arms and services but reliance had to be placed on Indian units until the Burmese units were formed and trained, and even then Indian personnel had to be employed in them for a time. Indian units which remained in Burma were in roughly the same position as British units, being 'on loan' to the Government of Burma.

The Burma Army used the same rank designations as the Indian Army.

(e) Navy and Air Force.

With the exception of a few units of the Royal Indian Navy and Burma Navy and one squadron of the Indian Air Force, all naval and air units during the 1942 campaign were provided and commanded by the Royal Navy and the Royal Air Force.

Police Organisation

In the early days of British rule the District Magistrate was also the Chief Police Officer. He was assisted by the 'Darogha' who was, originally, the Mogul official charged with law and order and the suppression of crime. The 'Darogha' was a man of substance and in these early days recruited his own police, often from a very low strata of society. He did some good service but his methods were not scientific and relied on 'strong arm' methods and a liberal use of the stick. Later the Government of India reorganised the Police and created an officer class, originally recruited from Army officers. These officers wore uniforms and badges of rank very similar to those of the Service from which they had come. The rank and file were recruited from the villages and were not men of education and it became imperative to have an intermediate type of officer to carry out the normal methods of detection and prevention of crime. This led to a three tier structure of Gazetted Officers, Subordinate Officers and rank and file; curious by British standards but in tune with the educational background and social structure of India and Burma. A man who entered as a Constable would rise no higher than Head Constable in normal circumstances. A man of some education could join direct in the subordinate officer rank, as a probationary Sub-Inspector and would retire, normally, as an Inspector. However, as an incentive, a few Inspectors were promoted to Gazetted Rank as Deputy Superintendents and even to Superintendent. The officer class entered direct after a Civil Service examination, as Assistant Superintendents. The Sergeant was recruited prior to 1947, entirely from Anglo-Indians/Anglo-Burmese. and were only found in large cities where there was a large European population.

The Police were Government servants and the Inspector-General was responsible to the Provincial Government for the administration and training of his force but had no executive functions. The executive officer was the Superintendent, who commanded the Police in his District, subject to the overall control of the District Magistrate. The poor educational standard of the Constables meant that they were used only for beat work, crowd and traffic control but all crime detection was done by the Sub-Inspectors and Inspectors, in fact, the work done in England by ranks from Detective Constable to Station Sergeant was, in India and Burma, done by the Inspector and Sub-Inspector grade. The four major cities of India – Calcutta, Bombay, Madras and including Rangoon – had separate Police Forces, and came directly under the Home Department of the Provincial Government and not under the Inspector General of Police or District Magistrate. The Gazetted Officers were seconded from the ordinary Police and in Rangoon, the Commissioner was of the rank of Deputy Inspector General; the Deputy and Assistant Commissioners and Superintendent Port Police were Superintendents and the attached Officer, an Assistant Superintendent.

APPENDIX B

Copies of Correspondence concerning alleged requisitions of Beer, etc., in Rangoon

No. P-12504/XX/Claims
Headquarters, Burma Army,
SIMLA,   1 July 1943

Major A. A. Mains,
GSO II (Intelligence),
IV Corps,
c/o No. 6 Advance Base Post Office,
INDIA.

A claim has been preferred by Messrs Barnett Bros Ltd, late of RANGOON, in which they state that they have received information from Mr F. R. TURNER, lately released from service with the Burma Army, that acting under orders issued by you in your capacity as Assistant Military Commandant, RANGOON, he removed more than 700 cases of beer, the property of the claimants, from a godown at No. 6/8 Campbell Road, RANGOON, during the last few days of February and the early days of March 1942. Mr TURNER is alleged to have informed the claimants that the final clearance was made about the 2nd or 3rd March, that he counted up to 700 cases and then stopped counting, but that more than that number were actually taken over, and that the beer was distributed, still under your orders, to various units such as the 7th Hussars, Cameronians, 17th Division then in the RANGOON area. No receipts were taken from the various units for the supplies.

The claimants have submitted a claim for the value of 700 cases UB and Queen Brand beer @ Rs 48/- per case.

This Headquarters has been directed by the Government of Burma to obtain verification of the number of cases of beer removed and their value. Will you, accordingly, be so good as to furnish the required information.

Captain,
for AA & QMG, Burma Army.

CHD/DRS

COPY

No. 5302/4 GSI (x),
HQ 202 L of C Area,
C/o No. 6 Adv. Base PO
Dated 12 July 1943

To   HQ BURMA ARMY,
    SIMLA.

Subject: CLAIMS.

Ref your No. P-12504/XX/Claims dated 1 July 1943.

1. The fact that the UB & Queen Brand Beer was removed from the godown in 6/8 Campbell Rd is correct.
2. There are other facts however which have not been mentioned:

(a) At the time in question, RANGOON had been evacuated and no member of the staff of M/S BARNETT Bros remained or returned in or to RANGOON.

(b) That I was given orders for the Security of RANGOON and in particular to secure all stocks of liquor to prevent looting, riot and arson.

(c) That when I heard of the godown at Campbell Rd I proceeded there and found that it had been broken into, about 30 or 40 cases had been looted and that several drunken Chinese were sprawled about the premises.

(d) For the furtherance of the object given in para (b)

above and to allow of these stores being put to use, I had the cases removed to the Supply Depot from where they were, I believe, issued in a proper orderly fashion.

(e) The godown was a small one and could not have contained more than 200 cases, I estimate that about 120 were removed. It is possible that Lt TURNER was counting all the liquor cases which were removed from other firms in addition and were in some cases put into the Reserve Bank Vaults for safe keeping.

(f) I am unaware of the policy of such claims but I will say without hesitation that (a) M/S BARNETT Bros had evacuated themselves leaving the beer behind. (b) If it had not been removed by me it would have been either looted or in the end taken over by the enemy.

Major,
General Staff.

GC/12.7.43

COPY   No. WRINoDO/INV/4229

From R. B. Groves, Esq.,   To Major A. A. Mains,
      The Executive Officer,
        Govt of Burma War Risks (Goods)
          Insurance Office,
     Wynnstay Lodge, SIMLA.

Simla, dated the 31st May 1944

My dear Mains,

Lower Poozooandaung

In the course of investigating a claim by Steels for Rice looted ex the Lower Poozooandaung Mill, Frank Turner has sworn an affidavit in which he has stated that on or about the 25th February 1942 he was one of a patrol of Police and Military which went to investigate a report of looting in the Poozooandaung area. On arrival at Burma Co. Ltd, Mill, they found a crowd of Burmans and Indians removing rice by carts and by hand. The crowd attempted to disperse but about 20 were arrested and confined in the local Police Station. He goes on to say that to the best of his recollection,

Major A. A. Mains, 9 Gurkha Rifles, Assistant Military Commandant, Rangoon, was in this Patrol.

Can you remember anything about this? If so, I would be very grateful to have your remarks, which would assist this Board in adjudicating upon the claim.

Yours sincerely,

(Sgd) R. B. Groves.

COPY   No. 565/1/GSI(b),
                                         HQ Fourteenth Army,
                                         C/o No. 12 ABPO,
                                         INDIA   19 June 44

Dear

With reference to your DO WRI/No.DO/INV/4229 of 31 May.

I can confirm 2/Lt TURNER'S remarks. Subsequent to 24 Feb., I was working as Asst Military Commandant of RANGOON and had been placed in charge of law and order. 2/Lt TURNER was under my orders.

I remember proceeding to the POOZOOANDAUNG Mill of Messrs STEEL Bros and arresting various native civilians who had looted rice and had loaded it on carts.

I visited this Mill almost daily with a patrol until the final evacuation, and can say that it was considerably looted as it was too far out of the centre of RANGOON for us to police effectively during the 'E' label and 'final warning' period.

(A. A. MAINS Major)

GII(Ib)

R. B. GROVES Esq.,
Executive Officer,
Govt of Burma War Risks (Goods) Insurance Office,
WYNNSTAY LODGE, SIMLA.
AAM.JK

APPENDIX C

Copies of Correspondence concerning Mr Ebbe Munch and his gold

Extract from a letter dated the 15th December 1942 from the Royal Danish Consulate, Bombay, to the Secretary to the Government of Burma, Defence Department.

I have the honour to refer to your letter informing me that you had received from the Government of India the cheques and currency notes as mentioned therein belonging to Mr Ebbe Munch. The insured parcel containing these cheques and currency notes was received by me only yesterday, and I now send you herewith my formal receipt for them.

2.   I may draw your attention to the fact that in the receipt given to Mr Munch by Lt-Col. V. Robert a copy of which receipt had already been sent to you, items 5, 6 and 7 mention gold dollar pieces of the total value of $100. Probably the $60 which you mention as having not been received are part of these being items 6 & 7. The balance of $40 being item 5 in the receipt I have received from you in the form of currency notes, and not as gold dollar pieces which was how it was deposited by Mr Munch. I shall therefore be much obliged if you will kindly inquire further in the matter.

No. 4790/23/G
HQ Burma Army,
Simla.   2 Feb 43.

To:

Major A. A. MAINS,
   GSOII(I),
     IV Corps,
       6 Adv. Base P.O.

We should be grateful for your comments on para 2 of the above letter, and the attached.

Lieut-Colonel,
General Staff, Burma Army

COPY

January 15th 43
PRI/E/270
Field

To:

Headquarters Burma Army,
     Simla.

Subject:

INTELLIGENCE

Ref your letter No. 4790/G dated 8/1/43 and my wire of today, the previous communications 19 Nov. and 26th December 42, have not reached me. I am making enquiries from the Imperial Bank of India, Calcutta, regarding these.

I confirm that a sum of money of various foreign currencies and securities were handed over to me for safe custody at the BI Depot, Maymyo, at the time Mr Ebbe Munch was confined to the cells by an officer of I Branch. He was eventually released about the 20th April and all the money handed back in the presence of a Major from I Branch accompanied by Lt Jilks of the FSS. I cannot say whether the officer was Major Widdicombe. I believe that Major Mains was dealing with this case and would be able to confirm. I hold no receipt in this respect.

Sd/- Chas M. Fox
Capt.
PRI
2/KOYLI

COPY

> No. 302/4/G'T'(x),
> Gauhati Int Dett.,
> c/o Postmaster, GAUHATI,
> 8th Feb., 1943.

To: HQ Burma Army,
    SIMLA.

Subject:

Mr EBBE MUNCH

Reference your No. 4790/23/G dated 2 Feb., 1943

1. To the best of my knowledge M. E. MUNCH was originally arrested by the Chinese forces in KENG TUNG for improperly crossing the Indo-China–Burma frontier. He was subsequently sent to MAYMYO where he was a Civil Security prisoner but for convenience was lodged in a military guard room.

2. I was aware that,

  (a) MUNCH had a large sum of money.

  (b) That originally this had included gold, but as to whether or not the gold accompanied him to MAYMYO, I cannot remember. I was of the opinion that it had been retained in KENG TUNG.

3. I issued orders for an FSS party to take MUNCH and his possessions from MAYMYO to SHWEBO but I was not present when he was handed over to his escort, as I was on duty at MAYMYO Railway Station.

4. I suggest that enquiries be made of,

> Lt-Col. STEWART,
> DIG Police Burma,
> Head of Burma Defence Bureau,

as he was in charge of this case.

> Major,
> OC, Int Dett

JH

APPENDIX D

Statement issued by Lieutenent-General N. M. S. Irwin on the arrival of the Burma Army in India, May 1942

'Now that the Burma Army is withdrawing into India, the duty of reorganising and re-equipping that army falls to a large extent on the headquarters of the corps under my command, a duty which is gladly accepted, but in view of the great difficulties and the shortness of time, I am conscious that there are, and will continue to be, many shortcomings in the arrangements now being made. I must therefore emphasise that the speed with which the troops will settle into the camps, which they will largely have to make themselves, will depend on themselves.

The reclothing and re-equipping of troops will also take time, and while this is going on, every step must be taken to reorganise units into their former selves, to complete records, lists of casualties and, at the same time, to fit the troops physically and by training for any task which may suddenly present itself.

The general policy for the reorganisation of the Burma Army will be as follows:

On account of the possibility of the enemy following up the withdrawal, it is essential to retain within the corps a sufficiency of troops to deal with the threat. This can only be done by retaining the major part of the fighting portion of the Burma Army until the situation on this front permits any redistribution of troops. It will not be possible, until available figures are known, to decide how best to reorganise the divisions, but in principle it will, of course, be our object to retain the identity of the division as before, and the units and formations in them.

As undoubtedly there will be a desire to know how long the formations may remain in the forward area, and of the appropriate plans and arrangements to be made, it will be expected that this will be until some time after the breaking of the monsoon, and every effort must accordingly be made, and will be made in so far as Corps Headquarters is concerned, to build accommodation as appropriate as possible to the climatic conditions which are to be expected, but it must be realised that this will take time and further hardships will have to be borne.

It will also be asked whether leave may be expected. The answer to this will depend on the military situation, but, again, it may be expected that should the situation justify it, and not unless, a small leave concession within India is likely to be granted. We must beat the enemy before we can think of leave.

At regards personnel and units of the Burma Army and corps troops, in general these will leave my corps area as soon as reasonably rested and re-equipped for the inward journey into India.

On the other hand, the resources of my corps are inadequate to meet the many demands placed on it by the circumstances of the arrival of the Burma Army and by the flow of refugees, and it therefore will be necessary, as it has been already, to retain the services of certain officers and other ranks and units forming part of corps and army troops to assist in the reorganising of the divisions.

I would like to close by saying that I am aware that the Burma Army has received the commendation of His Excellency the Commander-in-Chief, and therefore I know that after a rest the fighting qualities of the troops will be revived, and I can have confidence in believing that we should now, assisted by the monsoon and by the country over which we are deployed, be able finally to stop the invader, but this confidence is based on the fact that the difficult task of re-organising and recreating the divisions into their former selves shall be undertaken with the greatest speed and deter-mination. The immediate future will certainly be uncomfort-able and difficult, but I rely on commanders competing with each other in bringing their units up again to a high state of fighting efficiency within the shortest time so as to be ready for the next round, and on all ranks contributing towards this end by their own patience under trying conditions, and determination finally to defeat any enemy whom they must know is in no way superior to them.'

APPENDIX E

DRAMATIS PERSONAE

Officers of the British, Indian and Burma Armies

General Sir Archibald Wavell, Supreme Commander American, British, Dutch and Australian Command, later as Field-Marshal Lord Wavell, Viceroy of India.

Lieutenant-General The Honourable H. A. L. Alexander, GOC-in-C Burma Army; later Supreme Commander Middle East and Italy and, as Field-Marshal The Viscount Alexander KG, Governor-General of Canada.

Lieutenant-General T. J. Hutton, British Service GOC-in-C Burma until superseded by General Alexander.

Lieutenant-General N. M. S. Irwin, British Service, GOC-in-C IV Corps, later GOC-in-C Eastern Army (India).

Lieutenant-General William Slim, 6th Gurkha Rifles Indian Army, Commander Bur-corps, later GOC-in-C 14th Army and as Field-Marshal The Viscount Slim KG, Chief of the Imperial General Staff and Governor-General of Australia.

Major-General (later Lieutenant-General) E. N. Goddard, Indian Army, later GOC 202 L of C Area, Chief Administrative Officer Eastern Army and 11th Army Group and finally GOC-in-C Southern Command India.

Major-General J. G. Smyth, VC Indian Army, GOC 17th Indian Division. General Smyth won his VC in France in 1915.

Major-General A. V. T. Wakeley, British Service, GOC Line of Communication Burma.

Major-General T. J. W. Winterton, British Service, Major-General, General Staff Burma Army.

Brigadier (later Major-General) H. L. Davies, 18th Royal Garhwal Rifles, Indian Army, Brigadier General Staff Burma Army and later of Bur-corps.

Lieutenant-Colonel (later Brigadier) T. W. Boyce, 14th Punjab Regiment, Indian Army, GSOI(I) Iraq Force.

Lieutenant-Colonel (later Brigadier) P. F. C. J. Gwyn, 14th Punjab Regiment, Indian Army, GSOI Intelligence Burma Army.

Lieutenant-Colonel (later Brigadier) W. R. Selby, 9th Gurkha Rifles, Indian Army.

Major (later Brigadier) J. M. Calvert, Royal Engineers Officer Commanding The Bush Warfare School, Maymyo, later a column commander in Wingate's Chindit expeditions.

Major (later Colonel) J. C. Campbell, Royal Indian Army Service Corps – Commandant The Intelligence School.

Major D. E. Crowther, Kings Royal Rifle Corps (60th Rifles), GSO II Operations Burma Army.

Major J. G. Evans, The Dorset Regiment, GSO II I(a) Burma Army.

Major L. D. Gates, 13th Frontier Force Rifles, Indian Army, GSO II I(c) Burma Army.

Major A. A. Mains, 9th Gurkha Rifles, Indian Army, GSO II I(b) Burma Army.

Major B. F. Montgomery, 10th Baluch Regiment, Indian Army, GSO II Operations Burma Army.

Major P. H. D. Panton, 2nd King Edward VIIs Own Gurkha Rifles, Indian Army, DA & QMG 253 L of C Sub Area Manipur Road.

Major G. T. Widdicombe, 9th Gurkha Rifles, Indian Army, GSO II I(x) Burma Army.

Captain S. R. Acomb, Army in Burma Reserve of Officers, Field Security Officer.

Captain P. L. Leefe, Intelligence Corps, GSO III I(b) IV Corps.

Captain D. MacGilp, 5th Royal Gurkha Rifles, Indian Army, Field Security Officer.

Captain J. K. Majumdar, 16th Light Cavalry, Indian Army, Instructor Class C Intelligence School (India).

Captain Mansfield – Field Security Officer. It is regretted that Captain Mansfield cannot be identified in current Army lists. He was originally a Warrant Officer of the Army Educational Corps.

Captain L. A. Summersell, The Seaforth Highlanders, Field Security Officer.

Captain W. L. Talbot, Queens Own Regiment (West Surrey), GSO III I(b) Burma Army.

Lieutenant R. Ramamirthan, Army in Burma Reserve of Officers – Attached Officer GSI Branch Burma Army.

Officers of the American and Chinese Armies

Lieutenant-General J. W. Stilwell, US Army, Chief of Staff Chinese National Army later Commander China Burma & India Command US Army and Deputy Supreme Commander South East Asia.

Major-General Sun Li Jen, Chinese National Army – a graduate of the Virginia Military Academy and the most competent of the Chinese Generals.

Officers of the Burma Civil and Police Services

The Right Honourable Sir Reginald Dorman Smith, PC, Governor of Burma – a former Minister of Agriculture in Britain.

Mr D. C. P. Phelips, Indian Civil Service, Secretary Defence Department Government of Burma.

Mr C. G. Stewart, Indian Police, Deputy Inspector General of Police, Head of the Burma Defence Bureau.

Mr R. G. Prescott, Indian Police, Commissioner of Police Rangoon, later Inspector General of Police Burma in exile and on return to Burma in 1945.

Mr F. G. Bestall, Indian Police, Deputy Commissioner of Police Rangoon.

Mr W. H. Tydd, Indian Police, Assistant Commissioner of Police Rangoon.

Mr T. P. F. Fforde, Indian Police, Superintendent Port Police Rangoon.

Mr N. G. P. Hoole, Indian Police, Attached Officer (Assistant Superintendent) Rangoon.

Lieutenant-Colonel C. P. Brewitt, Burma Railway Service.

Sergeant Rivers, Mandalay District Police – attached to GS(Ib) Branch Burma Army.

War Correspondents

Mr Marsland Gander – *Daily Telegraph*.

Mr Alfred Wagg – American Correspondent – author of 'A Million Died'.

NEL BESTSELLERS

Crime

T012 484	FIVE RED HERRINGS	*Dorothy L. Sayers*	40p
T015 556	MURDER MUST ADVERTISE	*Dorothy L. Sayers*	40p
T014 398	STRIDING FOLLY	*Dorothy L. Sayers*	30p

Fiction

T015 386	THE NORTHERN LIGHT	*A. J. Cronin*	50p
T016 544	THE CITADEL	*A. J. Cronin*	75p
T015 130	THE MONEY MAKER	*John J. McNamara Jr.*	50p
T013 820	THE DREAM MERCHANTS	*Harold Robbins*	75p
T018 105	THE CARPETBAGGERS	*Harold Robbins*	95p
T016 560	WHERE LOVE HAS GONE	*Harold Robbins*	75p
T013 707	THE ADVENTURERS	*Harold Robbins*	80p
T006 743	THE INHERITORS	*Harold Robbins*	60p
T009 467	STILETTO	*Harold Robbins*	30p
T015 289	NEVER LEAVE ME	*Harold Robbins*	40p
T016 579	NEVER LOVE A STRANGER	*Harold Robbins*	75p
T011 798	A STONE FOR DANNY FISHER	*Harold Robbins*	60p
T015 874	79 PARK AVENUE	*Harold Robbins*	60p
T011 461	THE BETSY	*Harold Robbins*	75p
T013 340	SUMMER OF THE RED WOLF	*Morris West*	50p

Historical

T013 758	THE LADY FOR RANSOM	*Alfred Duggan*	40p
T015 297	COUNT BOHEMOND	*Alfred Duggan*	50p
T010 279	MASK OF APOLLO	*Mary Renault*	50p
T014 045	TREASURE OF PLEASANT VALLEY	*Frank Yerby*	35p
T015 602	GILLIAN	*Frank Yerby*	50p

Science Fiction

T015 017	EQUATOR	*Brian Aldiss*	30p
T014 347	SPACE RANGER	*Isaac Asimov*	30p
T015 491	PIRATES OF THE ASTEROIDS	*Isaac Asimov*	30p
T016 331	THE CHESSMEN OF MARS	*Edgar Rice Burroughs*	40p
T013 537	WIZARD OF VENUS	*Edgar Rice Burroughs*	30p
T009 696	GLORY ROAD	*Robert Heinlein*	40p
T016 900	STRANGER IN A STRANGE LAND	*Robert Heinlein*	75p
T011 844	DUNE	*Frank Herbert*	75p
T012 298	DUNE MESSIAH	*Frank Herbert*	40p
T015 211	THE GREEN BRAIN	*Frank Herbert*	30p

War

T013 367	DEVIL'S GUARD	*Robert Elford*	50p
T015 505	THE LAST VOYAGE OF GRAF SPEE	*Michael Powell*	30p
T015 661	JACKALS OF THE REICH	*Ronald Seth*	30p
T012 263	FLEET WITHOUT A FRIEND	*John Vader*	30p

Western

T016 994	No. 1 EDGE – THE LONER	*George G. Gilman*	30p
T016 536	No. 5 EDGE – BLOOD ON SILVER	*George G. Gilman*	30p
T017 621	No. 6 EDGE – THE BLUE, THE GREY AND THE RED	*George G. Gilman*	30p
T014 479	No. 7 EDGE – CALIFORNIA KILLING	*George G. Gilman*	30p
T015 254	No. 8 EDGE – SEVEN OUT OF HELL	*George G. Gilman*	30p
T015 475	No. 9 EDGE – BLOODY SUMMER	*George G. Gilman*	30p

General

T011 763	SEX MANNERS FOR MEN	*Robert Chartham*	30p
W002 531	SEX MANNERS FOR ADVANCED LOVERS	*Robert Chartham*	25p
W002 835	SEX AND THE OVER FORTIES	*Robert Chartham*	30p
T010 732	THE SENSUOUS COUPLE	*Dr. 'C'*	25p

NEL P.O. BOX 11, FALMOUTH, TR10 9EN, CORNWALL

Please send cheque or postal order. Allow 10p to cover postage and packing on one book plus 4p for each additional book.

Name ....

Address ....

....

Title ....
(SEPTEMBER)